HAL E. NICHOLS

ATLAS OF
AMERICAN HISTORY

The Churchill Biography

Volume III, 'The Challenge of War', 1914–1916
Volume III, Documents, Parts I and II
Volume IV, 'The Stricken World', 1916–1922
Volume IV, Documents, Parts I, II and III
Volume V, 'The Prophet of Truth', 1922–1939
The Exchequer Years, Documents, 1924–1929
The Wilderness Years, Documents, 1929–1935
The Coming of War, Documents, 1936–1939
Volume VI, 'Finest Hour', 1939–1941
Volume VII, 'Road to Victory', 1941–1945
Volume VIII, 'World in Torment', 1945–1965 (*in preparation*)

Historical works

The Appeasers (with Richard Gott)
The European Powers 1900–1945
Churchill: A Photographic Portrait
Sir Horace Rumbold: Portrait of a Diplomat
Exile and Return: the Emergence of Jewish Statehood
Final Journey: The Fate of the Jews of Nazi Europe
Auschwitz and the Allies: the Politics of Rescue
The Jews of Hope: The Plight of Soviet Jewry Today
Jerusalem: Rebirth of a City, 1838–1898
Holocaust: A History of the Jews of Europe during the Second World War

Editions of documents

Britain and Germany Between the Wars
Plough My Own Furrow, The Life of Lord Allen of Hurtwood
Servant of India: Diaries of the Viceroy's Private Secretary
Churchill (Spectrum Books: Great Lives Observed)
Lloyd George (Spectrum Books: Great Lives Observed)

Atlases

Recent History Atlas, 1860–1960
British History Atlas
American History Atlas
Jewish History Atlas
First World War Atlas
The Arab-Israeli Conflict: Its History in Maps
The Jews of Arab Lands: Their History in Maps
The Jews of Russia: Their History in Maps
Jerusalem: Illustrated History Atlas
Imperial Russian History Atlas
Soviet History Atlas
Children's Illustrated Bible Atlas
Atlas of the Holocaust

ATLAS OF AMERICAN HISTORY

REVISED EDITION

MARTIN GILBERT

Fellow of Merton College, Oxford

Cartography by ARTHUR BANKS and TERRY BICKNELL

DORSET PRESS

Library of Congress Catalog Card Number: 71-85777

1985 Dorset Press

This edition published by Dorset Press,
a division of MARBORO BOOKS
Corp. by arrangement with the proprietor.
Originally published as *American History Atlas.*

American History Atlas was first published in Great Britain in 1968 by Weidenfeld and Nicolson, London

ISBN 0-88029-058-7
(Previously ISBN 0-88029-016-1)

Printed in the United States of America

1 2 3 4 5 6 7 8 9 10

Preface

The idea for this atlas came to me while I was teaching at the University of South Carolina. Its aim is to provide a short but informative visual guide to American history. I have tried to make use of maps in the widest possible way, designing each one individually, and seeking to transform statistics and facts into something easily seen and grasped. My material has been obtained from a wide range of historical works, encyclopaedias and newspaper reports. I have tried to be as comprehensive as possible, consistent with clarity; only the reader can judge if I have succeeded.

More than fifteen years have passed since the first publication of this atlas. It was a period marked first by the intensification and then by the ending of the Vietnam war, with more than 55,000 American dead. It was also a period marked by a substantial increase in the population of the United States, and continued immigration. This same period has seen the development of outer space as a region of defence policy. New maps cover these recent developments.

I am grateful in this new edition to the cartographic skills of Mr Terry Bicknell, and I should once more welcome any notice of errors and suggestions for further maps.

MARTIN GILBERT
5 February 1985, Merton College, Oxford

List of Maps

ATLAS OF
AMERICAN HISTORY

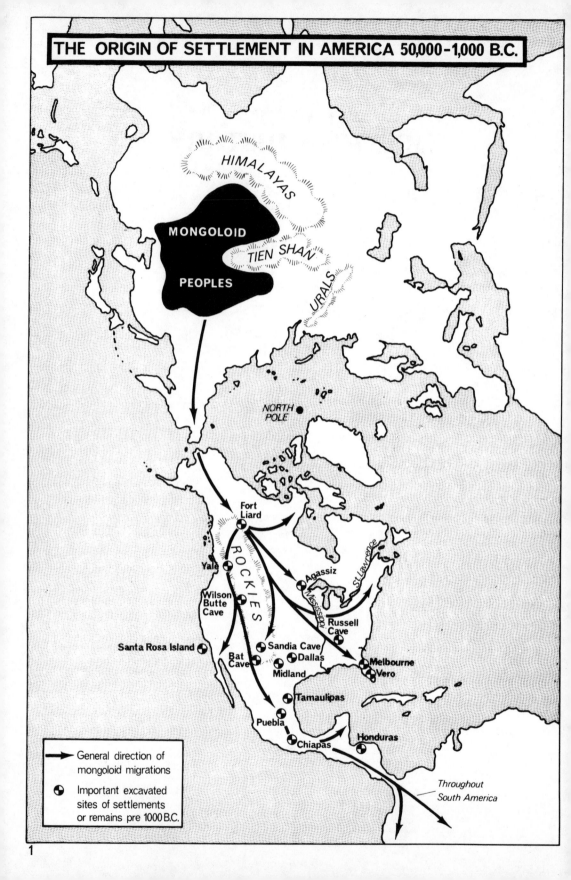

THE ORIGIN OF SETTLEMENT IN AMERICA 50,000–1,000 B.C.

HIMALAYAS

MONGOLOID

TIEN SHAN

PEOPLES

URALS

NORTH POLE

Fort Liard

ROCKIES

Yale

Wilson Butte Cave

Agassiz

Mississippi

St. Lawrence

Russell Cave

Santa Rosa Island

Bat Cave

Sandia Cave

Dallas

Midland

Melbourne

Vero

Tamaulipas

Puebla

Chiapas

Honduras

Throughout South America

General direction of mongoloid migrations

Important excavated sites of settlements or remains pre 1000 B.C.

THE INDIAN TRIBES OF NORTH AMERICA BEFORE 1492

Eskimo
Koyukon
Ingalik
Tanaina
Aleut

Kutchin
Han
Tanana
Nabesna
Tuchone
Ahtena
Kaska
Tahltan
Tlingit

Hare
Bear Lake
Dogrib
Yellowknife
Slave
Sekani
Beaver

Eskimo

Tsimshian
Bella Coola
Haida
Bella Bella
Kwakiutl
Nootka
Salish
Makah Puyallup
Nisqually
Chehalis
Chinook
Cowlitz
Tillamook
Yakima
Klikitat
Molala
Kalapuya
Coos
Umpqua
Takelma
Karok
Yurok
Wiyot
Shasta
Hupa
Yana
Mattole
Maidu
Yuki
Pomo
Wintun
Miwok
Costanoan
Yokuts
Salinan
Chumash

Carrier
Chilcotin
Shuswap
Lillooet
Thompson
Okanagan
Sanpoil
Colville
Spokane
Palouse
Walla Walla
Klamath
Modoc
Chomawi
Tsugewi
Kawaiisu
Mono
Panamint

Chipewyan

Sarsi
Siksika (Blackfoot)
Cree

Kaigani
Piegan
Kutenai
Kalispel
Atsina
Coeur D'Alene
Flathead
Crow
Nez Perce
Bannock
Shoshoni
Paviotso
Washo
Ute
Gosiute
S. Paiute
Navaho
Hopi
Zuni

Cayuse

N. Paiute

Hidatsa
Arikara
Teton
Yankton
Dakota
Ponca
Pawnee
N. Cheyenne
Arapaho
S. Cheyenne

Mandan

Santee Dakota

Mohave
Serpano
Yavapai
Cahuilla
Yuma
Pima
Maricopa
Papago

Kavasupai
Chemehuevi
Walapai
W. Apache
Lipan Apache
Cochimi
Seri

Ojibwa (Chippewa)
Ottawa
Plains Cree
Assiniboin

Jicarilla Apache
Pueblo
Kiowa
Kiowa Apache
Mescalero Apache
Tawakoni
Comanche
Kichai
Waco
Tonkawa

Iowa
Omaha
Oto
Kansa
Osage
Missouri
Quapaw

Naskapi Montagnais
Micmac
Malecite
Passamaquoddy
Penobscot
Abnaki
Huron

Beothuk

Pennacook

Mahican
Mohawk
Nipmuc Oneida
Massachuset
Wampanoag
Narraganset
Pequot
Mohegan
Wappinger
Onondaga
Cayuga
Seneca
Delaware
Nanticoke
Powhatan
Chickahominy
Mattapony
Tutelo
Pamlico
Nottoway
Tuscarora
Catawba

Tobacco
Neutral
Winnebago

Menomini
Sauk
Fox
Kickapoo
Miami
Wea
Peoria
Illinois
Shawnee
Yuchi
Cherokee

Erie

Potawatomie
Susquehanna
Pamunkey
Piankashaw

Choctaw Creek
Alabama
Chickasaw

Atakapa
Chitimacha
Biloxi
Mobile
Apalachee
Yucatan Maya

Tuskegee

Seminole

Caddo Natchez
Tunica

Opata
Tarahumara
Cahita
Acaxee

Concho
Coahuiltec
Tamaulipec
Huichol

Karankawa

Walcuri
Pericu
Yaqui

Rio Grande

Huastec

Yamasee
Guale
Timucua
Hichiti

Calusa

Taino

Ciboney

Toltec
Tarascan
Otomi

Totonac
Tlaxcalan
Aztec
Mixtec

Zapotec

Lacandon
Maya
Quiche
Maya

Mosquito

Chontal

There were approximately one million Indians north of Mexico in 1492

0   600
Miles

2

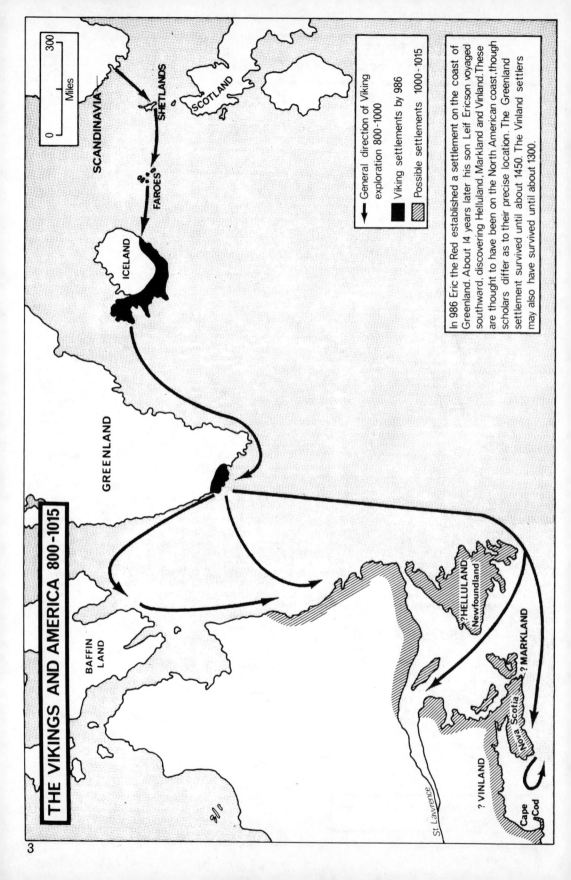

THE VIKINGS AND AMERICA 800-1015

SCANDINAVIA

SHETLANDS

SCOTLAND

FAROES

ICELAND

GREENLAND

BAFFIN LAND

St Lawrence

? HELLULAND
Newfoundland

? MARKLAND

Nova Scotia

? VINLAND

Cape Cod

0 — Miles — 300

General direction of Viking exploration 800-1000

Viking settlements by 986

Possible settlements 1000-1015

In 986 Eric the Red established a settlement on the coast of Greenland. About 14 years later his son Leif Ericson voyaged southward, discovering Helluland, Markland and Vinland. These are thought to have been on the North American coast, though scholars differ as to their precise location. The Greenland settlement survived until about 1450. The Vinland settlers may also have survived until about 1300.

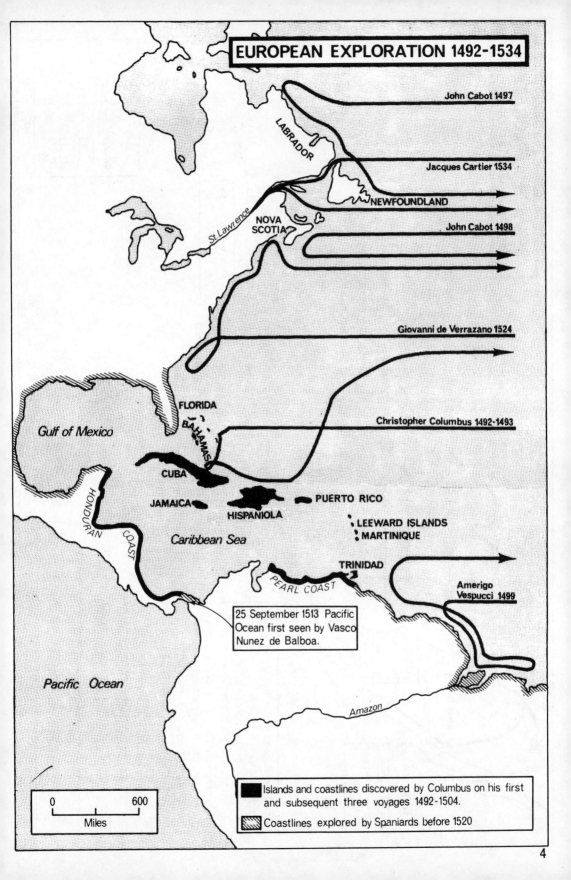

EUROPEAN EXPLORATION 1492-1534

John Cabot 1497

Jacques Cartier 1534

LABRADOR

NEWFOUNDLAND

John Cabot 1498

St.Lawrence

NOVA SCOTIA

Giovanni de Verrazano 1524

FLORIDA

BAHAMAS

Christopher Columbus 1492-1493

Gulf of Mexico

CUBA

JAMAICA

HISPANIOLA

PUERTO RICO

LEEWARD ISLANDS

MARTINIQUE

HONDURAN COAST

Caribbean Sea

TRINIDAD

PEARL COAST

Amerigo Vespucci 1499

25 September 1513 Pacific Ocean first seen by Vasco Nunez de Balboa.

Pacific Ocean

Amazon

Islands and coastlines discovered by Columbus on his first and subsequent three voyages 1492-1504.

Coastlines explored by Spaniards before 1520

0   600
Miles

4

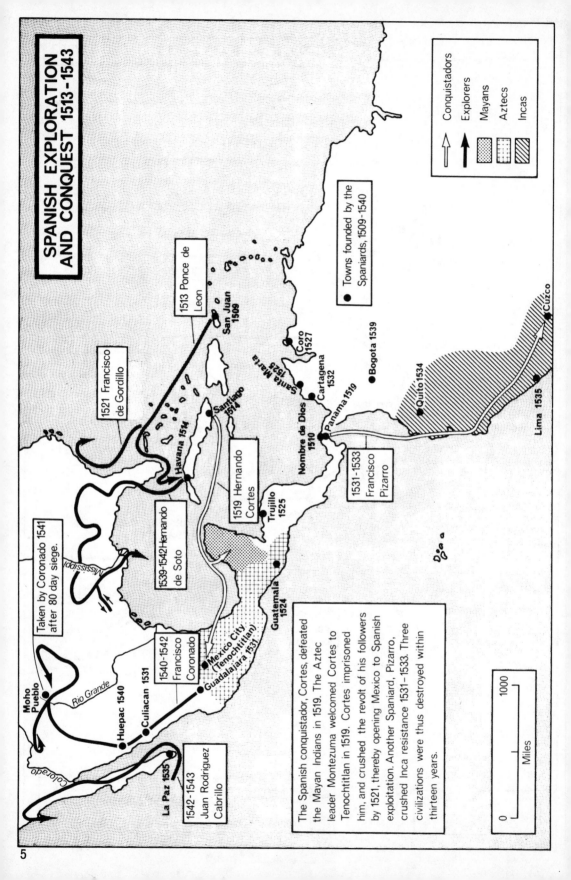

SPANISH EXPLORATION AND CONQUEST 1513-1543

Legend:
- Conquistadors
- Explorers
- Mayans
- Aztecs
- Incas
- ● Towns founded by the Spaniards, 1509-1540

1513 Ponce de Leon

1521 Francisco de Gordillo

San Juan 1509

Coro 1527

Santa Maria 1525

Cartagena 1532

Bogota 1539

Panama 1519

Nombre de Dios 1510

Quito 1534

Lima 1535

Cuzco

1531-1533 Francisco Pizarro

Havana 1514

Santiago 1514

1519 Hernando Cortes

Trujillo 1525

1539-1542 Hernando de Soto

Guatemala 1524

Mississippi

Taken by Coronado 1541 after 80 day siege.

Moho Pueblo

Rio Grande

Colorado

Huepac 1540

Culiacan 1531

1540-1542 Francisco Coronado

Mexico City (Tenochtitlan)

Guadalajara 1531

La Paz 1535

1542-1543 Juan Rodriguez Cabrillo

The Spanish conquistador, Cortes, defeated the Mayan Indians in 1519. The Aztec leader Montezuma welcomed Cortes to Tenochtitlan in 1519. Cortes imprisoned him, and crushed the revolt of his followers by 1521, thereby opening Mexico to Spanish exploitation. Another Spaniard, Pizarro, crushed Inca resistance 1531-1533. Three civilizations were thus destroyed within thirteen years.

0   Miles   1000

5

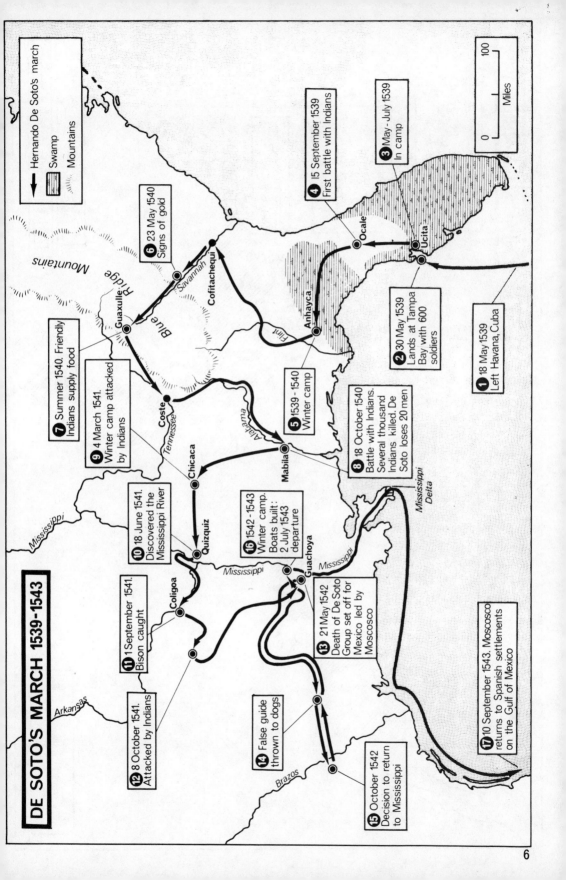

DE SOTO'S MARCH 1539-1543

Legend:
→ Hernando De Soto's march
Swamp
Mountains

Scale: 0 — 100 Miles

1 18 May 1539 Left Havana, Cuba

2 30 May 1539 Lands at Tampa Bay with 600 soldiers

3 May - July 1539 In camp

4 15 September 1539 First battle with Indians

5 1539 - 1540 Winter camp

6 23 May 1540 Signs of gold

7 Summer 1540. Friendly Indians supply food

8 18 October 1540 Battle with Indians. Several thousand Indians killed. De Soto loses 20 men

9 4 March 1541. Winter camp attacked by Indians

10 18 June 1541. Discovered the Mississippi River

11 1 September 1541. Bison caught

12 8 October 1541. Attacked by Indians

13 21 May 1542 Death of De Soto Group set off for Mexico led by Moscoso

14 False guide thrown to dogs

15 October 1542 Decision to return to Mississippi

16 1542 - 1543 Winter camp. Boats built: 2 July 1543 departure

17 10 September 1543. Moscoso returns to Spanish settlements on the Gulf of Mexico

Place names: Ucita, Ocale, Anhayca, Cofitachequi, Savannah, Guaxulle, Blue Ridge Mountains, Coste, Chicaca, Quizquiz, Coligoa, Guachoya, Mabila

Rivers: Mississippi, Tennessee, Alabama, Flint, Brazos, Arkansas, Mississippi Delta

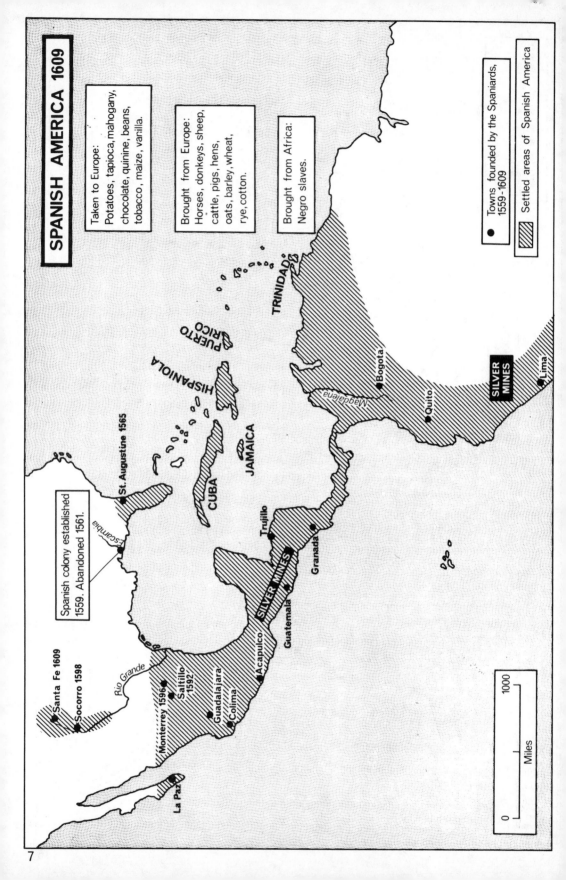

SPANISH AMERICA 1609

Taken to Europe:
Potatoes, tapioca, mahogany, chocolate, quinine, beans, tobacco, maize, vanilla.

Brought from Europe:
Horses, donkeys, sheep, cattle, pigs, hens, oats, barley, wheat, rye, cotton.

Brought from Africa:
Negro slaves.

● Towns founded by the Spaniards, 1559-1609

Settled areas of Spanish America

Spanish colony established 1559. Abandoned 1561.

Escambia

St. Augustine 1565

PUERTO RICO

HISPANIOLA

TRINIDAD

JAMAICA

CUBA

Bogota

Magdalena

Quito

Lima

SILVER MINES

Trujillo

Granada

Guatemala

SILVER MINES

Acapulco

Colima

Guadalajara

Saltillo 1592

Monterrey 1596

Rio Grande

Santa Fe 1609

Socorro 1598

La Paz

0   1000
Miles

7

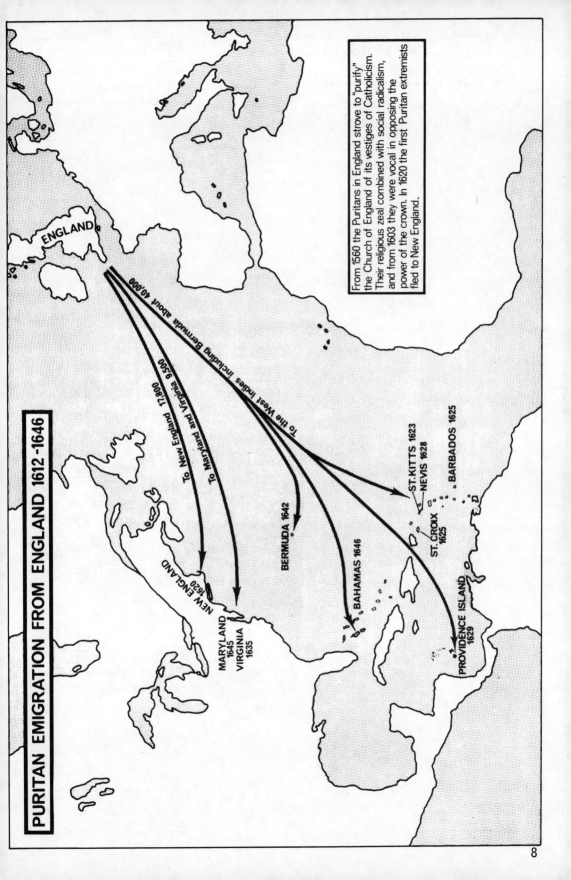

PURITAN EMIGRATION FROM ENGLAND 1612-1646

ENGLAND

From 1560 the Puritans in England strove to "purify" the Church of England of its vestiges of Catholicism. Their religious zeal combined with social radicalism, and from 1603 they were vocal in opposing the power of the crown. In 1620 the first Puritan extremists fled to New England.

To New England and Virginia 8,500

To Maryland and Virginia 17,800

To the West Indies including Bermuda about 40,000

NEW ENGLAND 1620

MARYLAND 1645
VIRGINIA 1635

BERMUDA 1642

BAHAMAS 1646

ST. KITTS 1623
NEVIS 1628

BARBADOS 1625

ST. CROIX 1625

PROVIDENCE ISLAND 1629

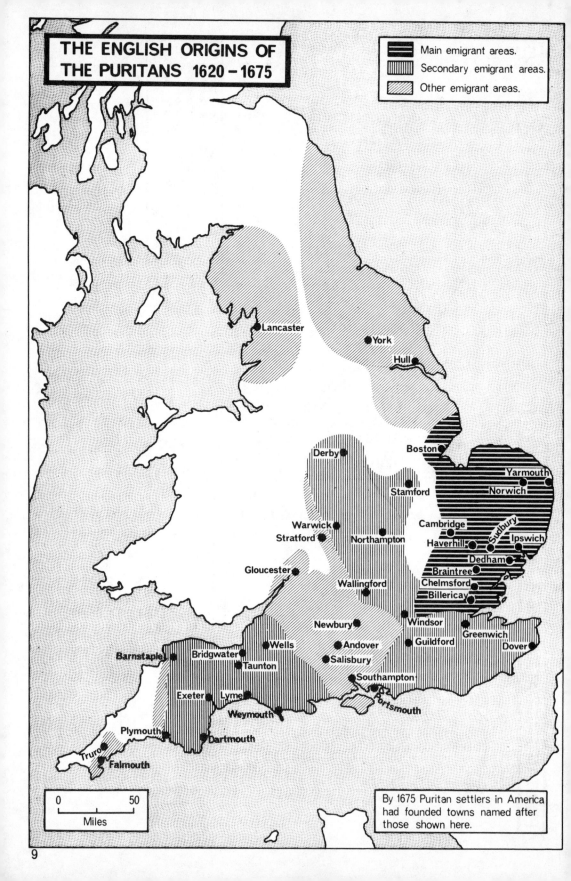

THE ENGLISH ORIGINS OF THE PURITANS 1620–1675

Main emigrant areas.
Secondary emigrant areas.
Other emigrant areas.

Lancaster

York

Hull

Derby

Boston

Yarmouth

Stamford

Norwich

Warwick
Stratford

Cambridge

Sudbury

Northampton

Haverhill

Ipswich

Dedham

Gloucester

Braintree

Wallingford

Chelmsford

Billericay

Newbury

Windsor

Andover

Guildford

Greenwich

Barnstaple

Bridgwater

Wells

Salisbury

Dover

Taunton

Southampton

Exeter

Lyme

Portsmouth

Weymouth

Plymouth

Dartmouth

Truro

Falmouth

0   50
Miles

By 1675 Puritan settlers in America had founded towns named after those shown here.

9

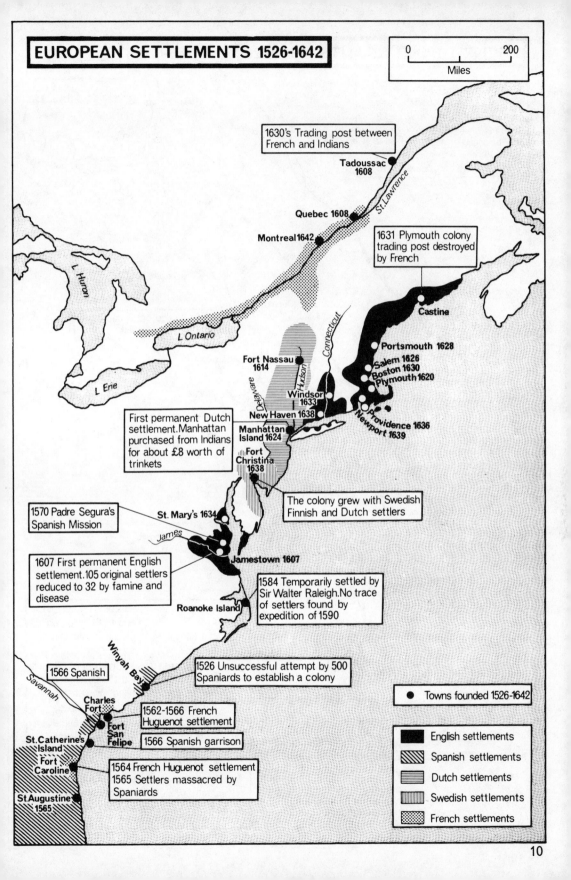

EUROPEAN SETTLEMENTS 1526-1642

0   200

Miles

1630's Trading post between French and Indians

Tadoussac 1608

Quebec 1608

St. Lawrence

Montreal 1642

1631 Plymouth colony trading post destroyed by French

Castine

L. Huron

L. Ontario

L. Erie

Portsmouth 1628

Fort Nassau 1614

Connecticut

Hudson

Salem 1626
Boston 1630
Plymouth 1620

Windsor 1633

Delaware

New Haven 1638

Providence 1636

First permanent Dutch settlement. Manhattan purchased from Indians for about £8 worth of trinkets

Manhattan Island 1624

Newport 1639

Fort Christina 1638

The colony grew with Swedish Finnish and Dutch settlers

1570 Padre Segura's Spanish Mission

St. Mary's 1634

James

1607 First permanent English settlement. 105 original settlers reduced to 32 by famine and disease

Jamestown 1607

1584 Temporarily settled by Sir Walter Raleigh. No trace of settlers found by expedition of 1590

Roanoke Island

Winyah Bay

1566 Spanish

1526 Unsuccessful attempt by 500 Spaniards to establish a colony

Savannah

Charles Fort

1562-1566 French Huguenot settlement

Fort San Felipe

1566 Spanish garrison

St. Catherine's Island

Fort Caroline

1564 French Huguenot settlement 1565 Settlers massacred by Spaniards

St. Augustine 1565

●   Towns founded 1526-1642

■   English settlements

■   Spanish settlements

■   Dutch settlements

■   Swedish settlements

■   French settlements

10

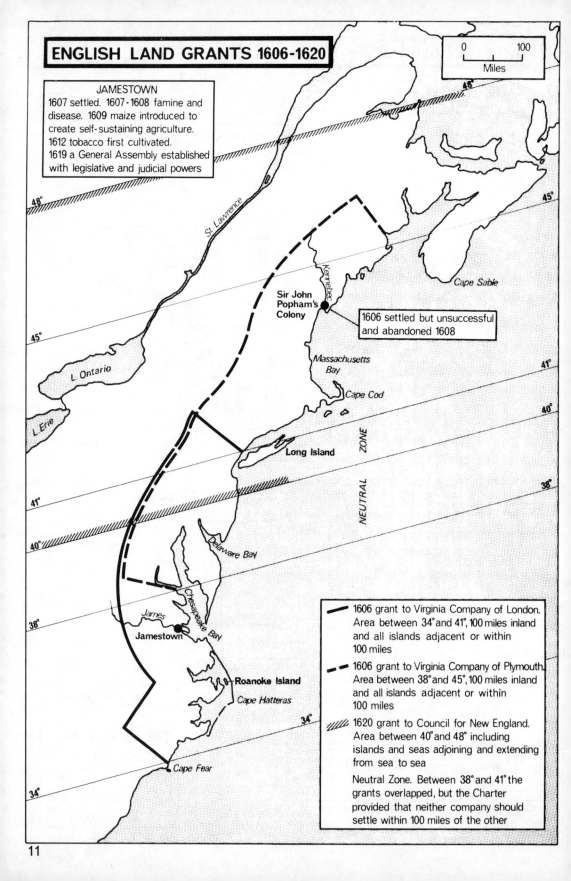

ENGLISH LAND GRANTS 1606-1620

0   100
Miles

JAMESTOWN
1607 settled. 1607-1608 famine and
disease. 1609 maize introduced to
create self-sustaining agriculture.
1612 tobacco first cultivated.
1619 a General Assembly established
with legislative and judicial powers

48°

45°

Sir John
Popham's
Colony

1606 settled but unsuccessful
and abandoned 1608

St. Lawrence

Kennebec

Cape Sable

Massachusetts
Bay

L. Ontario

45°

41°

40°

Cape Cod

L. Erie

Long Island

NEUTRAL   ZONE

41°

38°

40°

Delaware Bay

38°

James
Jamestown

Chesapeake Bay

Roanoke Island

Cape Hatteras

34°

34°

Cape Fear

— **1606** grant to Virginia Company of London.
Area between 34° and 41°, 100 miles inland
and all islands adjacent or within
100 miles

--- **1606** grant to Virginia Company of Plymouth.
Area between 38° and 45°, 100 miles inland
and all islands adjacent or within
100 miles

///// **1620** grant to Council for New England.
Area between 40° and 48° including
islands and seas adjoining and extending
from sea to sea

Neutral Zone. Between 38° and 41° the
grants overlapped, but the Charter
provided that neither company should
settle within 100 miles of the other

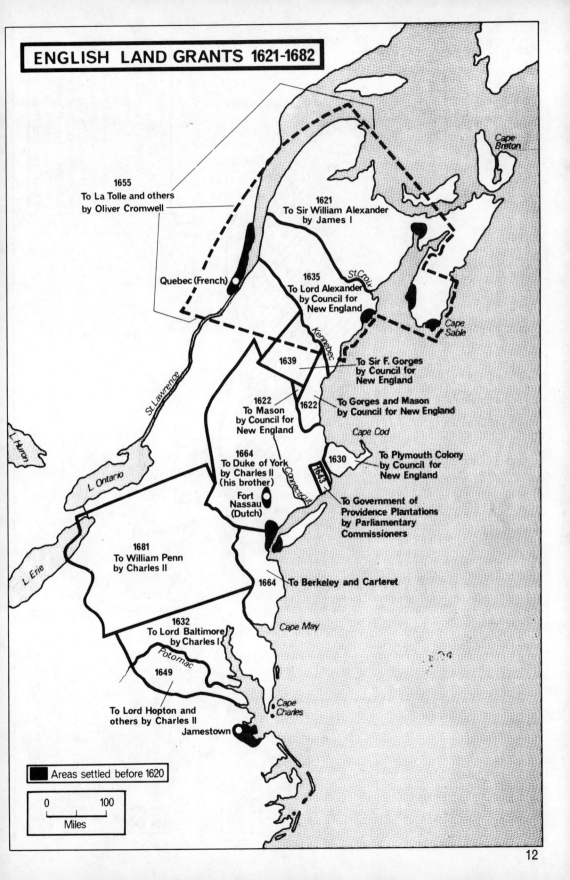

ENGLISH LAND GRANTS 1621-1682

1655
To La Tolle and others
by Oliver Cromwell

1621
To Sir William Alexander
by James I

Cape Breton

Quebec (French)

St Croix

1635
To Lord Alexander
by Council for
New England

Cape Sable

1639

To Sir F. Gorges
by Council for
New England

Kennebec

St. Lawrence

1622
To Mason
by Council for
New England

1622

To Gorges and Mason
by Council for New England

Cape Cod

L. Huron

1664
To Duke of York
by Charles II
(his brother)

1630

To Plymouth Colony
by Council for
New England

L. Ontario

Connecticut

1643

Fort
Nassau
(Dutch)

To Government of
Providence Plantations
by Parliamentary
Commissioners

1681
To William Penn
by Charles II

L. Erie

1664 To Berkeley and Carteret

Cape May

1632
To Lord Baltimore
by Charles I

Potomac

1649

Cape Charles

To Lord Hopton and
others by Charles II
Jamestown

■ Areas settled before 1620

0   100
├────┼────┤
Miles

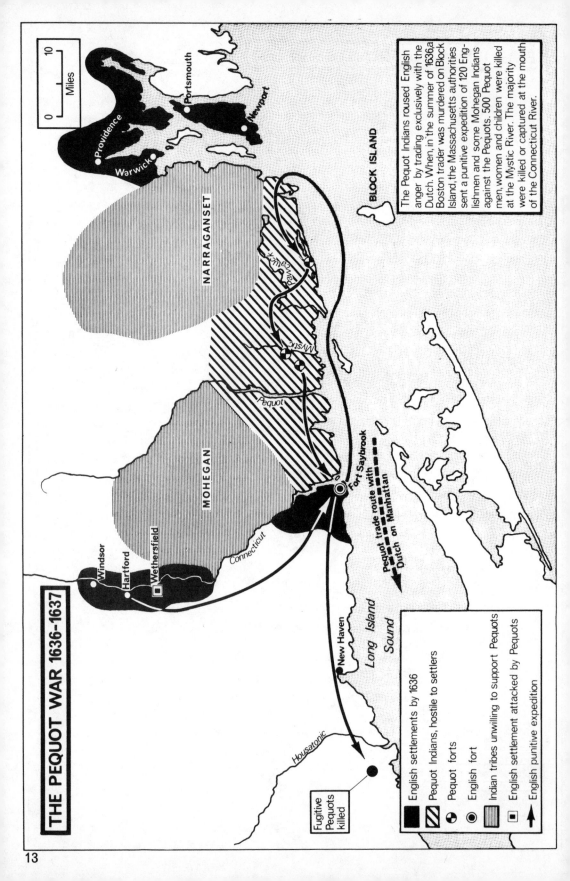

THE PEQUOT WAR 1636-1637

The Pequot Indians roused English anger by trading exclusively with the Dutch. When, in the summer of 1636, a Boston trader was murdered on Block Island, the Massachusetts authorities sent a punitive expedition of 120 Englishmen and some Mohegan Indians against the Pequots. 500 Pequot men, women and children were killed at the Mystic River. The majority were killed or captured at the mouth of the Connecticut River.

BLOCK ISLAND

NARRAGANSET

Portsmouth

Newport

Warwick

Providence

Pawcatuck

Mystic

Pequot

MOHEGAN

Fort Saybrook

Pequot trade route with Dutch on Manhattan

Connecticut

Windsor

Hartford

Wethersfield

New Haven

Long Island Sound

Housatonic

Fugitive Pequots killed

- English settlements by 1636
- Pequot Indians, hostile to settlers
- Pequot forts
- English fort
- Indian tribes unwilling to support Pequots
- English settlement attacked by Pequots
- English punitive expedition

Miles
0   10

13

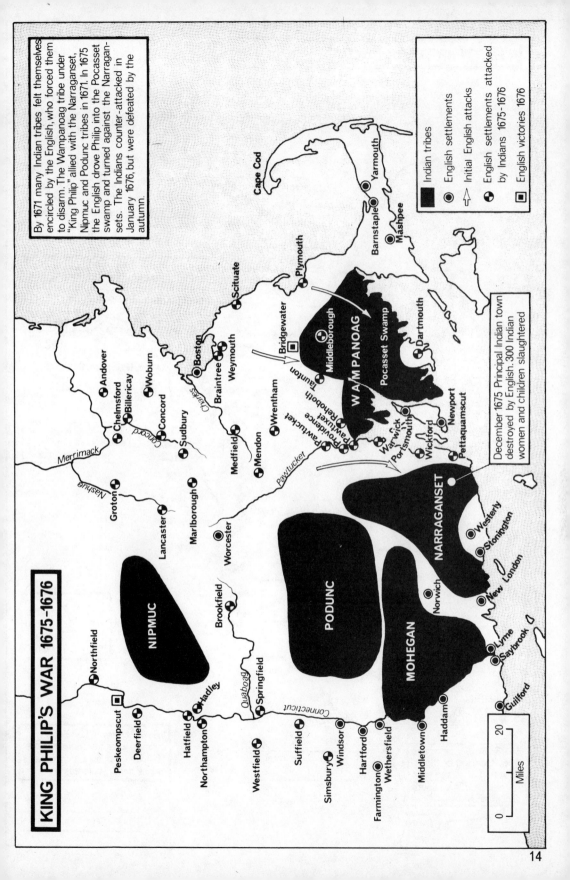

KING PHILIP'S WAR 1675-1676

By 1671 many Indian tribes felt themselves encircled by the English, who forced them to disarm. The Wampanoag tribe under "King Philip" allied with the Narraganset. In 1675 Nipmuc and Podunc tribes in 1671. In 1675 the English drove Philip into the Pocasset swamp and turned against the Narragansets. The Indians counter-attacked in January 1676, but were defeated by the autumn.

Indian tribes

● English settlements

⬆ Initial English attacks

◐ English settlements attacked by Indians 1675-1676

◼ English victories 1676

December 1675 Principal Indian town destroyed by English. 300 Indian women and children slaughtered

NIPMUC

PODUNC

MOHEGAN

NARRAGANSET

WAMPANOAG

Pocasset Swamp

Cape Cod

Northfield
Peskeompscut
Deerfield
Hatfield
Northampton
Westfield
Hadley
Springfield
Suffield
Simsbury
Windsor
Hartford
Farmington
Wethersfield
Middletown
Haddam
Guilford
Saybrook
Lyme
New London
Norwich
Stonington
Westerly
Pettaquamscut
Newport
Wickford
Portsmouth
Warwick
Providence
Pawtucket
Rehoboth
Mendon
Wrentham
Medfield
Marlborough
Worcester
Lancaster
Brookfield
Groton
Sudbury
Concord
Chelmsford
Billericay
Andover
Woburn
Braintree
Weymouth
Boston
Scituate
Bridgewater
Middleborough
Dartmouth
Barnstaple
Mashpee
Yarmouth
Plymouth
Taunton

Merrimack
Nashua
Concord
Charles
Pawtucket
Quaboag
Connecticut

20
0
Miles

14

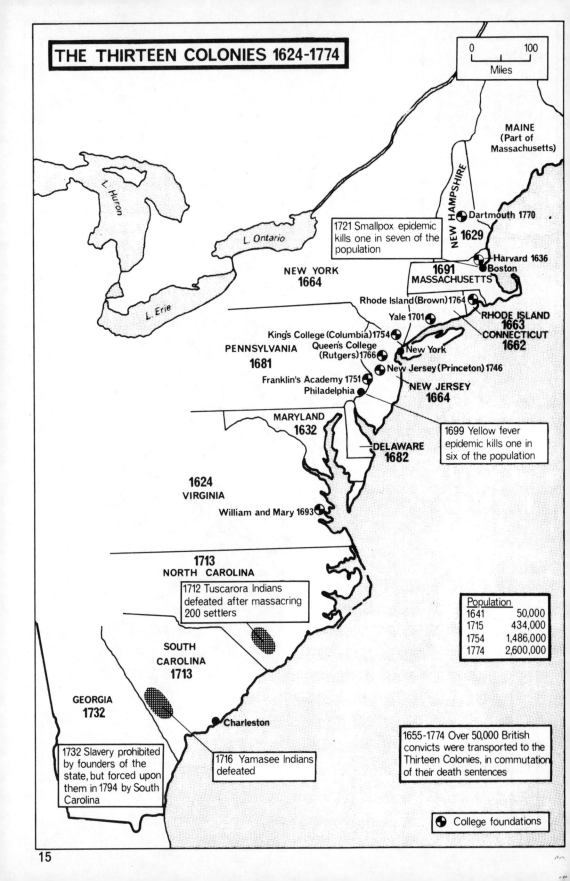

THE THIRTEEN COLONIES 1624-1774

0   100
Miles

MAINE
(Part of
Massachusetts)

L. Huron

L. Ontario

L. Erie

NEW HAMPSHIRE

Dartmouth 1770

1629

NEW YORK
1664

1721 Smallpox epidemic
kills one in seven of the
population

Harvard 1636
Boston

1691
MASSACHUSETTS

Rhode Island(Brown)1764

Yale 1701

RHODE ISLAND
1663
CONNECTICUT
1662

King's College (Columbia)1754

New York

PENNSYLVANIA
1681

Queen's College
(Rutgers)1766

New Jersey(Princeton)1746

Franklin's Academy 1751
Philadelphia

NEW JERSEY
1664

MARYLAND
1632

DELAWARE
1682

1699 Yellow fever
epidemic kills one in
six of the population

1624
VIRGINIA

William and Mary 1693

1713
NORTH CAROLINA

1712 Tuscarora Indians
defeated after massacring
200 settlers

SOUTH
CAROLINA
1713

GEORGIA
1732

Charleston

Population	
1641	50,000
1715	434,000
1754	1,486,000
1774	2,600,000

1732 Slavery prohibited
by founders of the
state, but forced upon
them in 1794 by South
Carolina

1716 Yamasee Indians
defeated

1655-1774 Over 50,000 British
convicts were transported to the
Thirteen Colonies, in commutation
of their death sentences

College foundations

CALIFORNIA MISSIONS 1769-1848

⊕ Missions established between 1769 and 1823

● Principal Spanish towns

In 1700 a Spanish Jesuit first established that California was not an island. The impetus to European settlement in California came from Spanish missionaries. In 1769 Spain formally occupied California; partly to forestall British designs. Los Angeles was founded in 1798.

The Missions contained in all over 15,000 Indians, trained by the priests in agriculture, wine-growing and livestock rearing. Under Spanish rule the Missions flourished. But in 1833 the Mexicans deprived the Church of its authority over the Missions. During the U.S.-Mexican war of 1848 the Indians were forced out of their Mission homes, which were occupied by U.S. soldiers and ranchers.

California Mission Livestock in 1811

Sheep	107,177
Cows & oxen	67,782
Horses	19,429
Mules	877

Population of California in 1848

Indians	24,000
Spanish-Mexicans	12,000
American traders and settlers	500

C A L I F O R N I A

Sierra Nevada

Solano 1823
San Rafael 1817
San Francisco 1776
San José 1797
Santa Clara 1777
San José
Santa Cruz 1791
San Juan Bautista 1797
San Carlos 1770
Monterey
Soledad 1771
San Antonio 1771
San Miguel 1797
San Louis Obispo 1772
La Purísima 1787
Santa Ynez 1804
Santa Barbara 1786
San Buenaventura 1782
San Fernando 1797
San Gabriel 1771
Los Angeles
San Juan Capistrano 1776
San Louis Rey 1798
San Diego 1769
Yuma 1780

Colorado

PACIFIC OCEAN

0 — 100
Miles

16

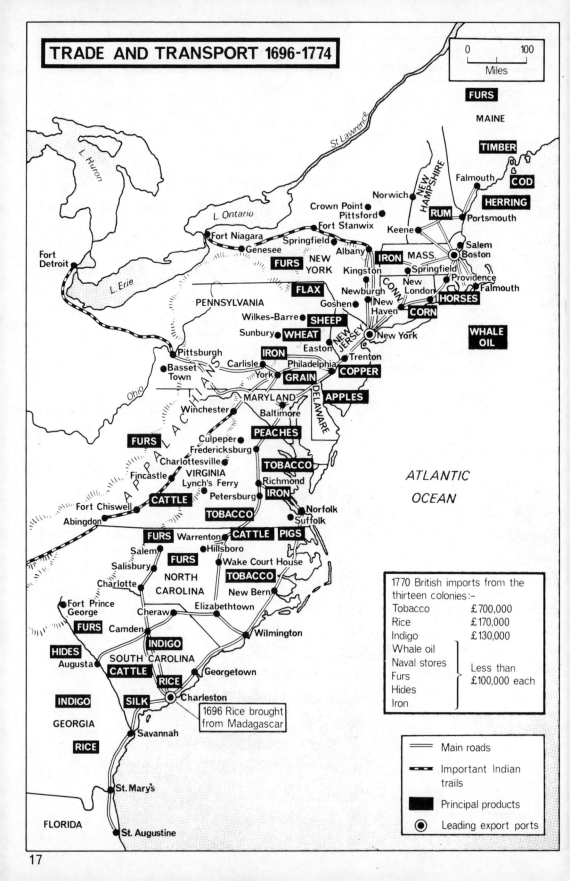

TRADE AND TRANSPORT 1696-1774

0   100
Miles

FURS

MAINE

TIMBER

Falmouth

COD

Norwich

HERRING

Crown Point

Pittsford

RUM

Portsmouth

NEW HAMPSHIRE

Fort Stanwix

Keene

Salem

L. Ontario

Fort Niagara

Springfield

Albany

IRON   MASS.

Boston

Genesee

Kingston

Springfield

Providence

Fort Detroit

L. Huron

FURS

NEW YORK

Newburgh

New London

Falmouth

FLAX

Goshen

New Haven

CONN.

HORSES

L. Erie

PENNSYLVANIA

Wilkes-Barre

SHEEP

CORN

Sunbury

WHEAT

NEW JERSEY

WHALE OIL

Pittsburgh

IRON

Easton

New York

Basset Town

Carlisle

Philadelphia

Trenton

Ohio

York

GRAIN

COPPER

Winchester

MARYLAND

APPLES

Baltimore

DELAWARE

Culpeper

PEACHES

FURS

Fredericksburg

Charlottesville

Fincastle

VIRGINIA

TOBACCO

Lynch's Ferry

Richmond

Petersburg

IRON

APPALACHIAN

Fort Chiswell

CATTLE

Abingdon

TOBACCO

Norfolk

Suffolk

FURS

Warrenton

CATTLE

PIGS

Salem

Hillsboro

Salisbury

FURS

Wake Court House

Charlotte

NORTH CAROLINA

TOBACCO

New Bern

Fort Prince George

Cheraw

Elizabethtown

FURS

Camden

Wilmington

HIDES

INDIGO

Augusta

SOUTH CAROLINA

CATTLE

Georgetown

RICE

INDIGO

SILK

Charleston

GEORGIA

1696 Rice brought from Madagascar

Savannah

RICE

St. Mary's

FLORIDA

St. Augustine

ATLANTIC OCEAN

1770 British imports from the thirteen colonies:-
Tobacco   £700,000
Rice   £170,000
Indigo   £130,000
Whale oil
Naval stores
Furs   } Less than
Hides   £100,000 each
Iron

———— Main roads

–■–■– Important Indian trails

■ Principal products

◉ Leading export ports

17

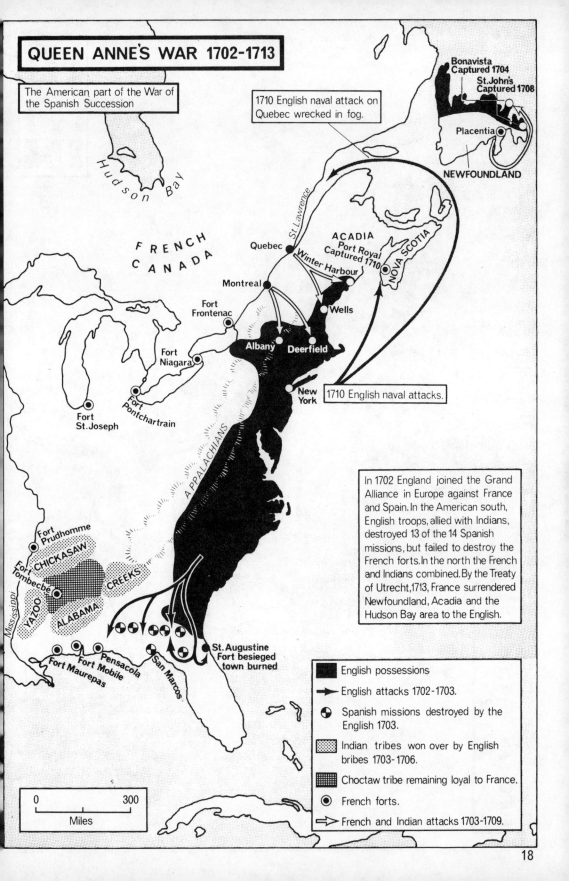

QUEEN ANNE'S WAR 1702-1713

The American part of the War of the Spanish Succession

1710 English naval attack on Quebec wrecked in fog.

Bonavista Captured 1704
St. John's Captured 1708
Placentia
NEWFOUNDLAND

Hudson Bay

St Lawrence

F R E N C H
C A N A D A

Quebec

ACADIA
Port Royal Captured 1710

Winter Harbour

NOVA SCOTIA

Montreal

Fort Frontenac

Wells

Fort Niagara

Albany Deerfield

Fort Pontchartrain

New York

1710 English naval attacks.

Fort St. Joseph

APPALACHIANS

In 1702 England joined the Grand Alliance in Europe against France and Spain. In the American south, English troops, allied with Indians, destroyed 13 of the 14 Spanish missions, but failed to destroy the French forts. In the north the French and Indians combined. By the Treaty of Utrecht, 1713, France surrendered Newfoundland, Acadia and the Hudson Bay area to the English.

Fort Prudhomme

Fort Tombecbe

CHICKASAW

CREEKS

ALABAMA

Mississippi

YAZOO

Fort Maurepas
Fort Mobile
Pensacola

San Marcos

St. Augustine Fort besieged town burned

◼ English possessions

➤ English attacks 1702-1703.

◉ Spanish missions destroyed by the English 1703.

▒ Indian tribes won over by English bribes 1703-1706.

▓ Choctaw tribe remaining loyal to France.

◉ French forts.

⇨ French and Indian attacks 1703-1709.

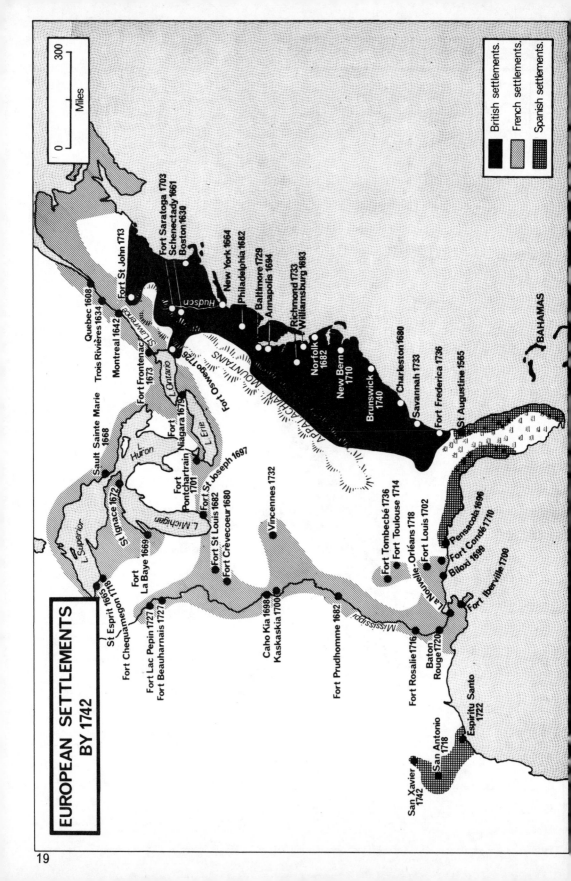

EUROPEAN SETTLEMENTS BY 1742

British settlements.
French settlements.
Spanish settlements.

0 — 300 Miles

Quebec 1608
Trois Rivières 1634
Montreal 1642
Fort Frontenac 1673
Sault Sainte Marie 1668
Fort Niagara 1679
St Esprit 1665
Fort Chequamegon 1718
St Ignace 1672
Fort La Baye 1669
Fort Lac Pepin 1727
Fort Beauharnais 1727
Fort Pontchartrain 1701
Fort St Louis 1682
Fort St Joseph 1697
Fort Crèvecoeur 1680
Vincennes 1732
Caho Kia 1698
Kaskaskia 1700
Fort Prudhomme 1682
Fort Rosalie 1716
Baton Rouge 1720
San Antonio 1718
San Xavier 1742
Espiritu Santo 1722

Fort St John 1713
Fort Saratoga 1703
Schenectady 1661
Boston 1630
New York 1664
Philadelphia 1682
Baltimore 1729
Annapolis 1694
Richmond 1733
Williamsburg 1693
Norfolk 1682
New Bern 1710
Brunswick 1740
Charleston 1680
Savannah 1733
Fort Frederica 1736
St Augustine 1565

Fort Tombecbé 1736
Fort Toulouse 1714
Fort Louis 1702
La Nouvelle Orléans 1718
Pensacola 1696
Fort Condé 1710
Biloxi 1699
Fort Iberville 1700

BAHAMAS

APPALACHIAN MOUNTAINS

L. Superior
Huron
L. Michigan
L. Erie
L. Ontario
Hudson
St. Lawrence
Mississippi

Fort Oswego 1726

19

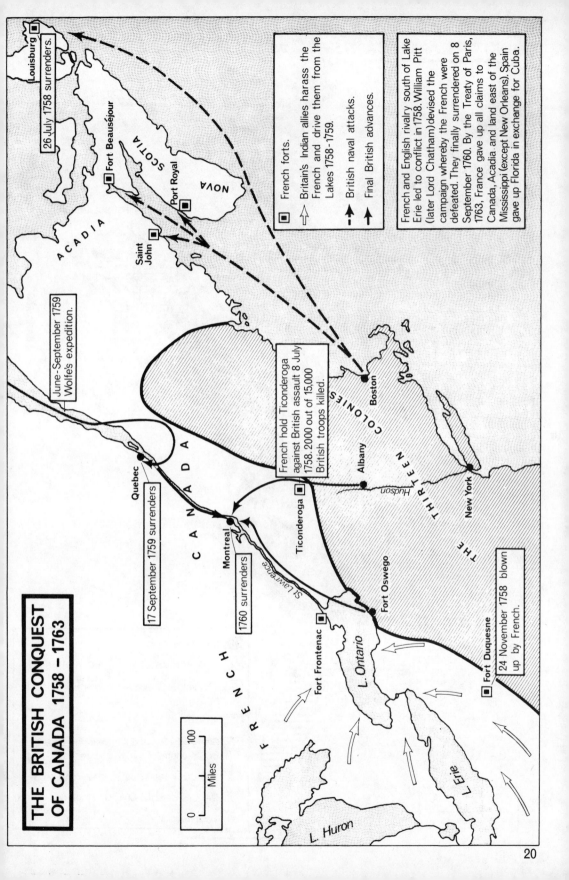

THE BRITISH CONQUEST OF CANADA 1758–1763

Louisburg

26 July 1758 surrenders.

ACADIA

Fort Beauséjour

NOVA SCOTIA

Port Royal

Saint John

French forts.

Britain's Indian allies harass the French and drive them from the Lakes 1758–1759.

British naval attacks.

Final British advances.

French and English rivalry south of Lake Erie led to conflict in 1758. William Pitt (later Lord Chatham) devised the campaign whereby the French were defeated. They finally surrendered on 8 September 1760. By the Treaty of Paris, 1763, France gave up all claims to Canada, Acadia and land east of the Mississippi (except New Orleans). Spain gave up Florida in exchange for Cuba.

June–September 1759 Wolfe's expedition.

French hold Ticonderoga against British assault 8 July 1758. 2000 out of 15,000 British troops killed.

Boston

Albany

Hudson

New York

THE THIRTEEN COLONIES

Quebec

17 September 1759 surrenders

CANADA

Montreal surrenders

1760 surrenders

St. Lawrence

Ticonderoga

FRENCH

Fort Oswego

Fort Frontenac

L. Ontario

Fort Duquesne

24 November 1758 blown up by French.

L. Erie

L. Huron

100

Miles

0

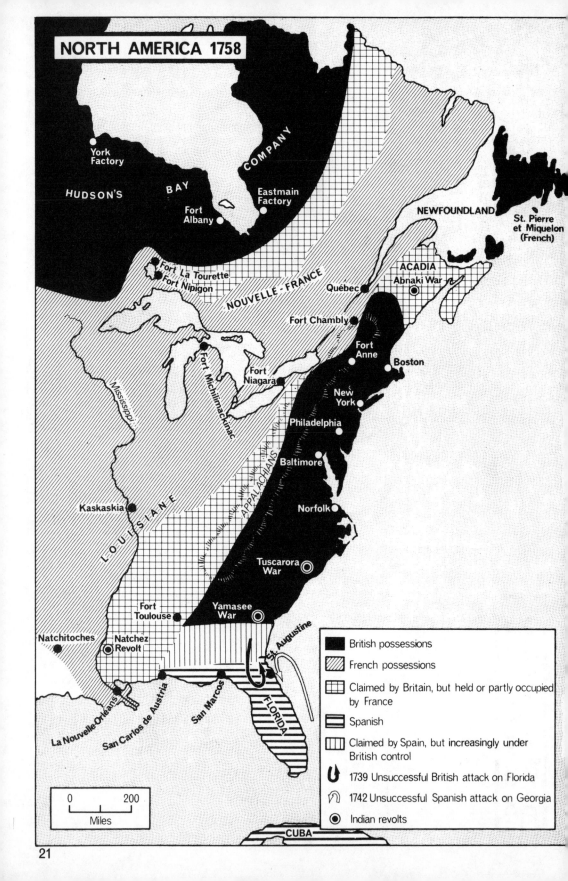

NORTH AMERICA 1758

York Factory

HUDSON'S BAY COMPANY

Fort Albany

Eastmain Factory

NEWFOUNDLAND

St. Pierre et Miquelon (French)

Fort La Tourette
Fort Nipigon

NOUVELLE - FRANCE

ACADIA

Québec

Abnaki War

Fort Chambly

Fort Michilimackinac

Fort Niagara

Fort Anne

Boston

New York

Mississippi

Philadelphia

APPALACHIANS

Baltimore

Kaskaskia

L O U I S I A N E

Norfolk

Tuscarora War

Yamasee War

Fort Toulouse

Natchitoches

Natchez Revolt

St. Augustine

La Nouvelle-Orléans

San Carlos de Austria

San Marcos

FLORIDA

■	British possessions
▨	French possessions
▦	Claimed by Britain, but held or partly occupied by France
▤	Spanish
▥	Claimed by Spain, but increasingly under British control
↶	1739 Unsuccessful British attack on Florida
⌂	1742 Unsuccessful Spanish attack on Georgia
◉	Indian revolts

0   200
Miles

CUBA

21

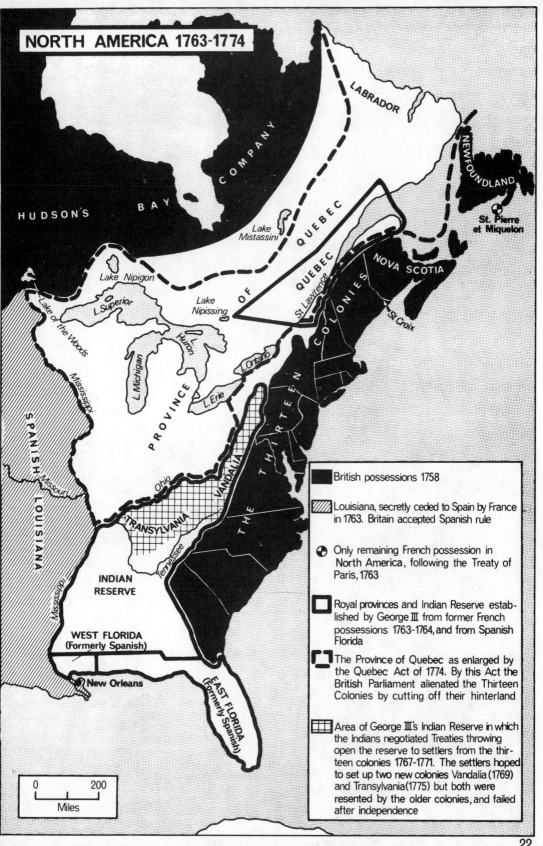

NORTH AMERICA 1763-1774

HUDSON'S BAY COMPANY

HUDSON'S BAY

LABRADOR

NEWFOUNDLAND

St. Pierre et Miquelon

Lake Mistassini

QUEBEC

PROVINCE OF QUEBEC

NOVA SCOTIA

St. Lawrence

St. Croix

Lake Nipigon

Lake of the Woods

L. Superior

Lake Nipissing

L. Huron

L. Michigan

L. Ontario

L. Erie

PROVINCE

Mississippi

Missouri

SPANISH LOUISIANA

Ohio

VANDALIA

TRANSYLVANIA

Tennessee

THE THIRTEEN COLONIES

INDIAN RESERVE

WEST FLORIDA (Formerly Spanish)

New Orleans

EAST FLORIDA (Formerly Spanish)

Mississippi

■ British possessions 1758

▨ Louisiana, secretly ceded to Spain by France in 1763. Britain accepted Spanish rule

⊕ Only remaining French possession in North America, following the Treaty of Paris, 1763

☐ Royal provinces and Indian Reserve established by George III from former French possessions 1763-1764, and from Spanish Florida

⌐┐ The Province of Quebec as enlarged by
└⌐ the Quebec Act of 1774. By this Act the British Parliament alienated the Thirteen Colonies by cutting off their hinterland

▦ Area of George III's Indian Reserve in which the Indians negotiated Treaties throwing open the reserve to settlers from the thirteen colonies 1767-1771. The settlers hoped to set up two new colonies Vandalia (1769) and Transylvania (1775) but both were resented by the older colonies, and failed after independence

0   200
Miles

22

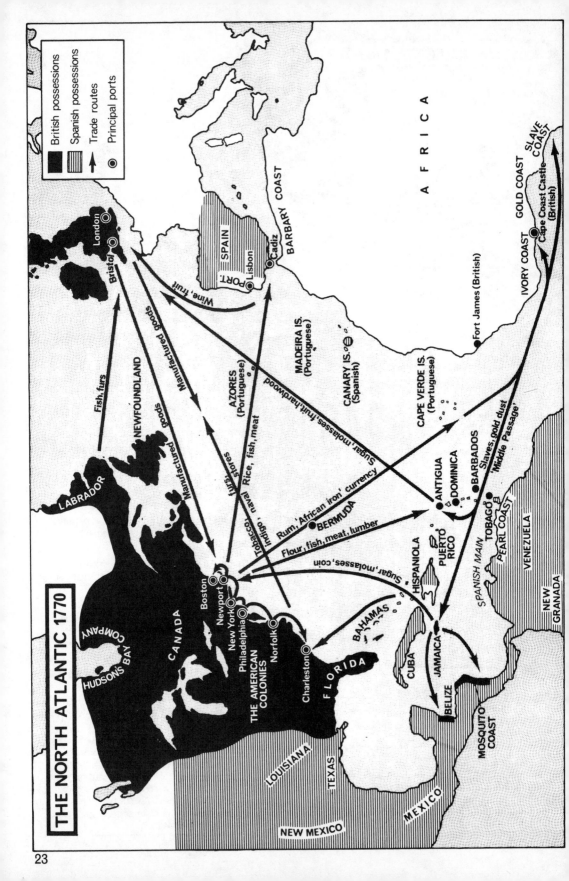

THE NORTH ATLANTIC 1770

British possessions
Spanish possessions
Trade routes
Principal ports

AFRICA

London
Bristol
SPAIN
PORT.
Lisbon
Cadiz
BARBARY COAST

SLAVE COAST
GOLD COAST
IVORY COAST
Cape Coast Castle (British)
Fort James (British)

Fish, furs
NEWFOUNDLAND
LABRADOR
HUDSON'S BAY COMPANY
CANADA

Manufactured goods
Manufactured goods
furs, stores
Tobacco, naval stores, 'iron' currency

Wine, fruit
AZORES (Portuguese)
MADEIRA IS. (Portuguese)
CANARY IS. (Spanish)
CAPE VERDE IS. (Portuguese)

Sugar, molasses, fruit, hardwood
Rice, fish, meat

Boston
Newport
New York
Philadelphia
Norfolk
THE AMERICAN COLONIES
Charleston
FLORIDA
BAHAMAS
BERMUDA

Rum, 'African iron' currency
Flour, fish, meat, lumber
Sugar, molasses, coin

Slaves, gold dust
'Middle Passage'

ANTIGUA
DOMINICA
BARBADOS
TOBAGO

HISPANIOLA
PUERTO RICO
CUBA
JAMAICA
SPANISH MAIN
PEARL COAST
VENEZUELA
NEW GRANADA

BELIZE
MOSQUITO COAST
MEXICO
TEXAS
LOUISIANA
NEW MEXICO

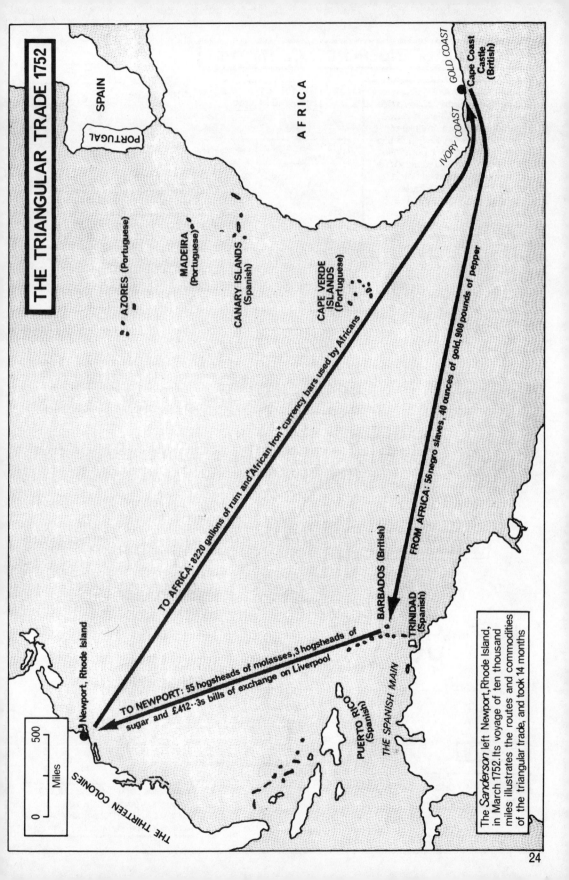

THE TRIANGULAR TRADE 1752

SPAIN

PORTUGAL

A F R I C A

GOLD COAST

Cape Coast
Castle
(British)

IVORY COAST

AZORES (Portuguese)

MADEIRA
(Portuguese)

CANARY ISLANDS
(Spanish)

CAPE VERDE
ISLANDS
(Portuguese)

TO AFRICA: 9220 gallons of rum and "African iron" currency bars used by Africans

FROM AFRICA: 56 negro slaves, 40 ounces of gold, 900 pounds of pepper

BARBADOS (British)

TRINIDAD
(Spanish)

PUERTO RICO
(Spanish)

THE SPANISH MAIN

Newport, Rhode Island

TO NEWPORT: 55 hogsheads of molasses, 3 hogsheads of
sugar and £412··3s bills of exchange on Liverpool

THE THIRTEEN COLONIES

500

Miles

0

The *Sanderson* left Newport, Rhode Island,
in March 1752. Its voyage of ten thousand
miles illustrates the routes and commodities
of the triangular trade, and took 14 months

24

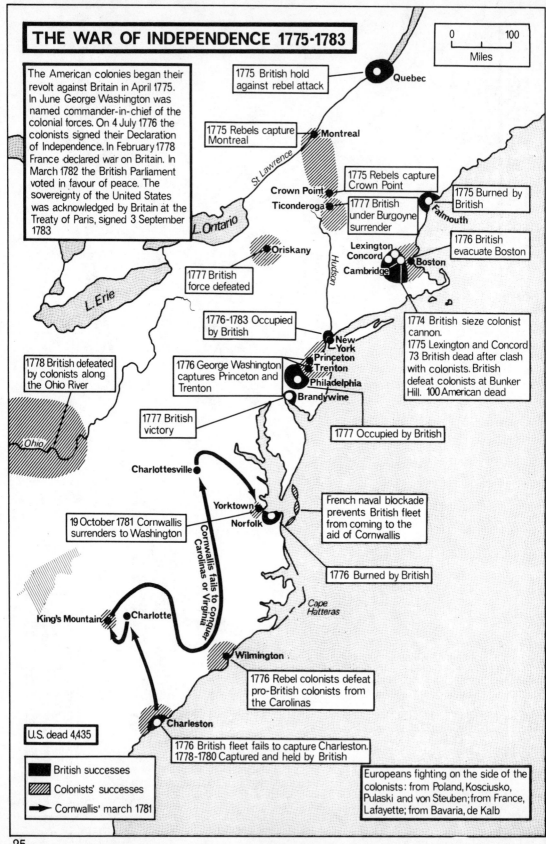

THE WAR OF INDEPENDENCE 1775-1783

0 _____ 100
Miles

The American colonies began their revolt against Britain in April 1775. In June George Washington was named commander-in-chief of the colonial forces. On 4 July 1776 the colonists signed their Declaration of Independence. In February 1778 France declared war on Britain. In March 1782 the British Parliament voted in favour of peace. The sovereignty of the United States was acknowledged by Britain at the Treaty of Paris, signed 3 September 1783

1775 British hold against rebel attack

Quebec

1775 Rebels capture Montreal

Montreal

St Lawrence

L Ontario

1775 Rebels capture Crown Point

Crown Point

Ticonderoga

1777 British under Burgoyne surrender

1775 Burned by British

Falmouth

Oriskany

1777 British force defeated

L. Erie

Lexington Concord

Cambridge

Boston

1776 British evacuate Boston

Hudson

1776-1783 Occupied by British

1778 British defeated by colonists along the Ohio River

Ohio

New York

Princeton
Trenton

Philadelphia

1776 George Washington captures Princeton and Trenton

Brandywine

1774 British sieze colonist cannon.
1775 Lexington and Concord 73 British dead after clash with colonists. British defeat colonists at Bunker Hill. 100 American dead

1777 British victory

1777 Occupied by British

Charlottesville

Yorktown

Norfolk

French naval blockade prevents British fleet from coming to the aid of Cornwallis

19 October 1781 Cornwallis surrenders to Washington

Cornwallis fails to conquer Carolinas or Virginia

1776 Burned by British

Cape Hatteras

King's Mountain

Charlotte

Wilmington

1776 Rebel colonists defeat pro-British colonists from the Carolinas

U.S. dead 4,435

Charleston

1776 British fleet fails to capture Charleston.
1778-1780 Captured and held by British

■ British successes

▨ Colonists' successes

➤ Cornwallis' march 1781

Europeans fighting on the side of the colonists: from Poland, Kosciusko, Pulaski and von Steuben; from France, Lafayette; from Bavaria, de Kalb

25

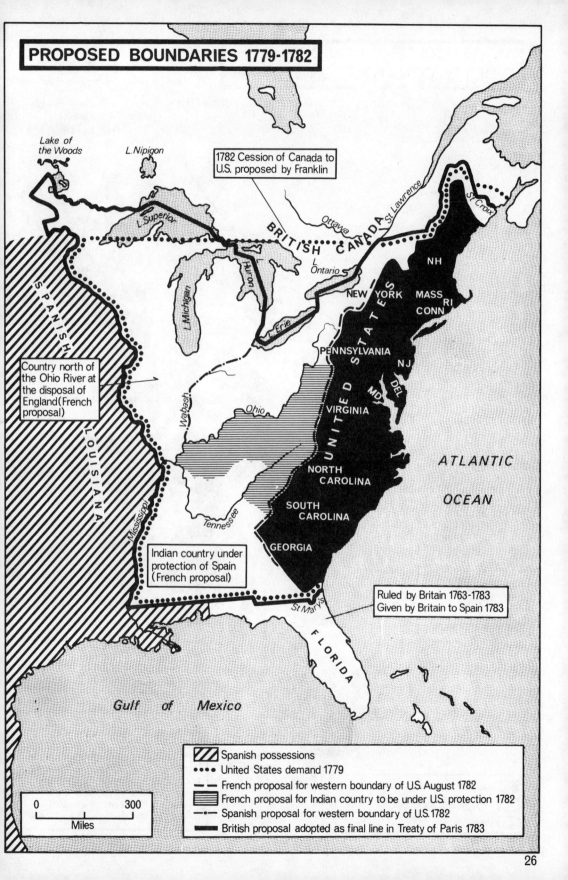

PROPOSED BOUNDARIES 1779-1782

Lake of the Woods

L. Nipigon

1782 Cession of Canada to U.S. proposed by Franklin

Ottawa

St. Lawrence

St. Croix

BRITISH CANADA

L. Superior

L. Huron

L. Michigan

L. Ontario

Erie

NH

NEW YORK

MASS

RI

CONN

S P A N I S H

Country north of the Ohio River at the disposal of England (French proposal)

PENNSYLVANIA

NJ

DEL

MD

Wabash

Ohio

VIRGINIA

U N I T E D   S T A T E S

L O U I S I A N A

NORTH CAROLINA

Tennessee

Mississippi

SOUTH CAROLINA

Indian country under protection of Spain (French proposal)

GEORGIA

ATLANTIC

OCEAN

St Mary's

Ruled by Britain 1763-1783 Given by Britain to Spain 1783

F L O R I D A

Gulf   of   Mexico

Spanish possessions
United States demand 1779
French proposal for western boundary of U.S. August 1782
French proposal for Indian country to be under U.S. protection 1782
Spanish proposal for western boundary of U.S. 1782
British proposal adopted as final line in Treaty of Paris 1783

0   300

Miles

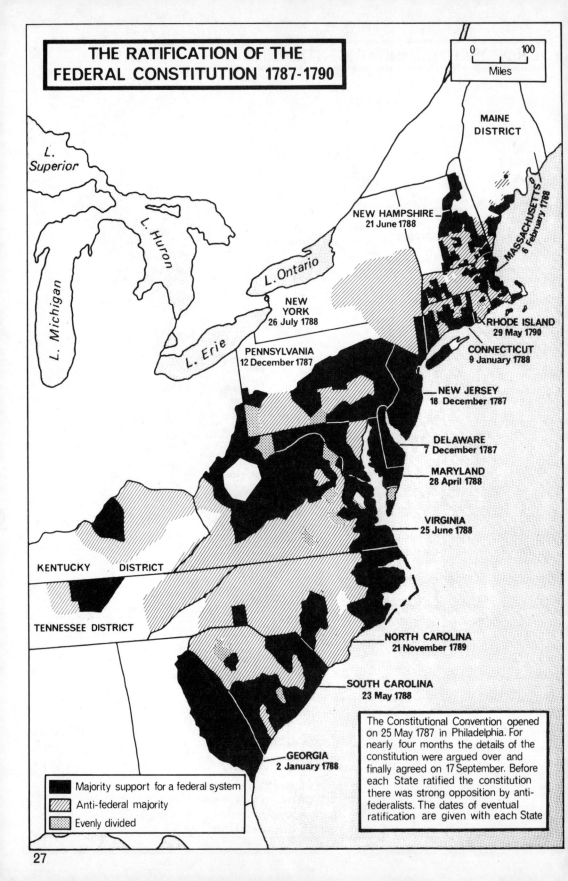

THE RATIFICATION OF THE FEDERAL CONSTITUTION 1787-1790

0   100
Miles

MAINE DISTRICT

L. Superior

L. Huron

L. Michigan

L. Ontario

L. Erie

NEW HAMPSHIRE
21 June 1788

MASSACHUSETTS
6 February 1788

NEW YORK
26 July 1788

RHODE ISLAND
29 May 1790

CONNECTICUT
9 January 1788

PENNSYLVANIA
12 December 1787

NEW JERSEY
18 December 1787

DELAWARE
7 December 1787

MARYLAND
28 April 1788

VIRGINIA
25 June 1788

KENTUCKY   DISTRICT

TENNESSEE DISTRICT

NORTH CAROLINA
21 November 1789

SOUTH CAROLINA
23 May 1788

GEORGIA
2 January 1788

The Constitutional Convention opened on 25 May 1787 in Philadelphia. For nearly four months the details of the constitution were argued over and finally agreed on 17 September. Before each State ratified the constitution there was strong opposition by anti-federalists. The dates of eventual ratification are given with each State

■ Majority support for a federal system

▨ Anti-federal majority

▦ Evenly divided

27

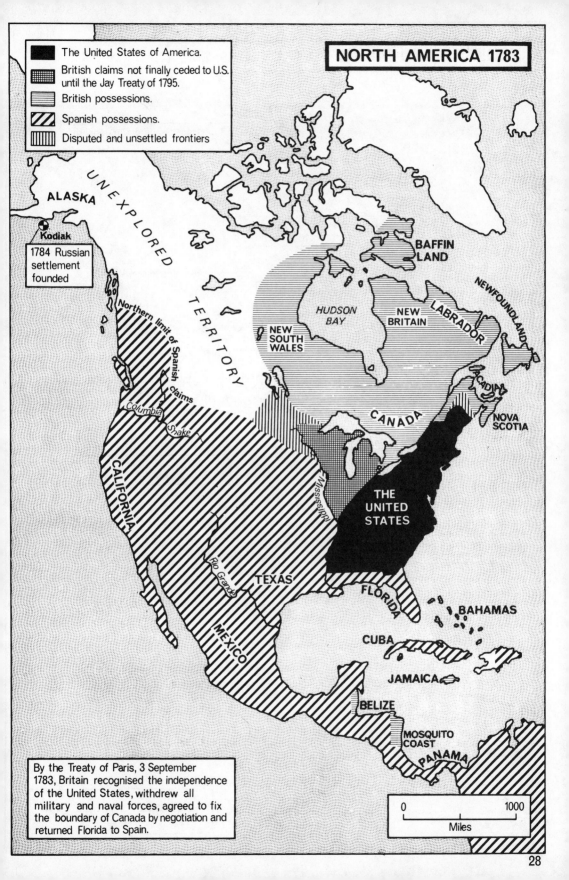

NORTH AMERICA 1783

The United States of America.

British claims not finally ceded to U.S. until the Jay Treaty of 1795.

British possessions.

Spanish possessions.

Disputed and unsettled frontiers

ALASKA

UNEXPLORED

Kodiak

1784 Russian settlement founded

Northern limit of Spanish claims

Columbia

Snake

TERRITORY

BAFFIN LAND

HUDSON BAY

NEW SOUTH WALES

NEW BRITAIN

LABRADOR

NEWFOUNDLAND

CANADA

ACADIA

NOVA SCOTIA

CALIFORNIA

Rio Grande

Mississippi

THE UNITED STATES

TEXAS

FLORIDA

BAHAMAS

MEXICO

CUBA

JAMAICA

BELIZE

MOSQUITO COAST

PANAMA

By the Treaty of Paris, 3 September 1783, Britain recognised the independence of the United States, withdrew all military and naval forces, agreed to fix the boundary of Canada by negotiation and returned Florida to Spain.

0   1000

Miles

28

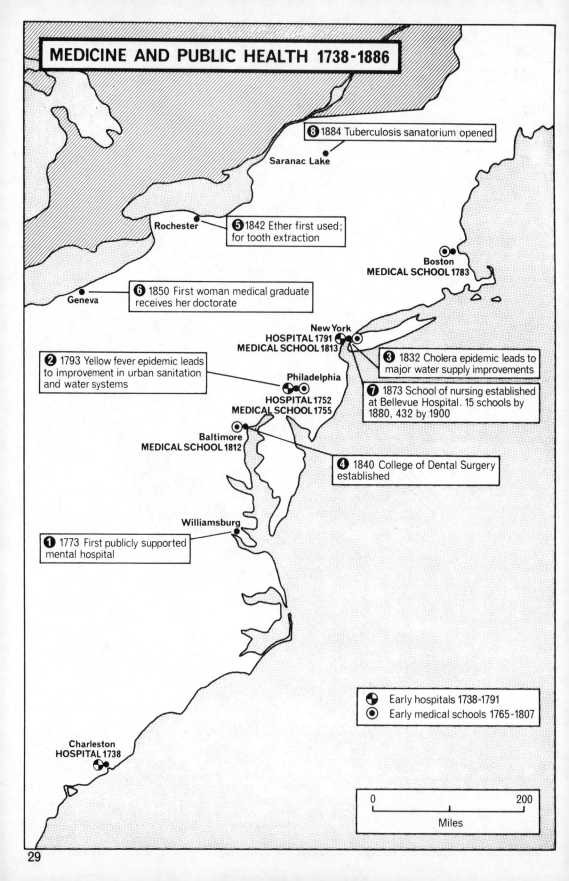

MEDICINE AND PUBLIC HEALTH 1738-1886

8 1884 Tuberculosis sanatorium opened

Saranac Lake

Rochester

5 1842 Ether first used; for tooth extraction

Boston
MEDICAL SCHOOL 1783

6 1850 First woman medical graduate receives her doctorate

Geneva

New York
HOSPITAL 1791
MEDICAL SCHOOL 1813

2 1793 Yellow fever epidemic leads to improvement in urban sanitation and water systems

3 1832 Cholera epidemic leads to major water supply improvements

Philadelphia
HOSPITAL 1752
MEDICAL SCHOOL 1755

7 1873 School of nursing established at Bellevue Hospital. 15 schools by 1880, 432 by 1900

Baltimore
MEDICAL SCHOOL 1812

4 1840 College of Dental Surgery established

Williamsburg

1 1773 First publicly supported mental hospital

	Early hospitals 1738-1791
	Early medical schools 1765-1807

Charleston
HOSPITAL 1738

0   200

Miles

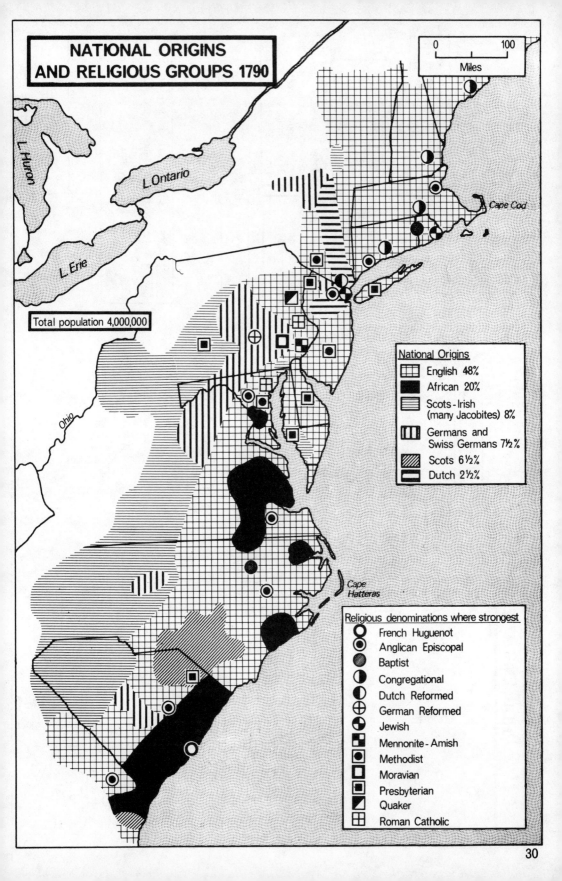

NATIONAL ORIGINS AND RELIGIOUS GROUPS 1790

0   100
Miles

L. Huron

L. Ontario

L. Erie

Cape Cod

Ohio

Total population 4,000,000

Cape Hatteras

National Origins

English 48%
African 20%
Scots-Irish (many Jacobites) 8%
Germans and Swiss Germans 7½%
Scots 6½%
Dutch 2½%

Religious denominations where strongest

◯	French Huguenot
◉	Anglican Episcopal
◐	Baptist
◑	Congregational
◑	Dutch Reformed
⊕	German Reformed
⊕	Jewish
▨	Mennonite - Amish
▣	Methodist
□	Moravian
▪	Presbyterian
◪	Quaker
⊞	Roman Catholic

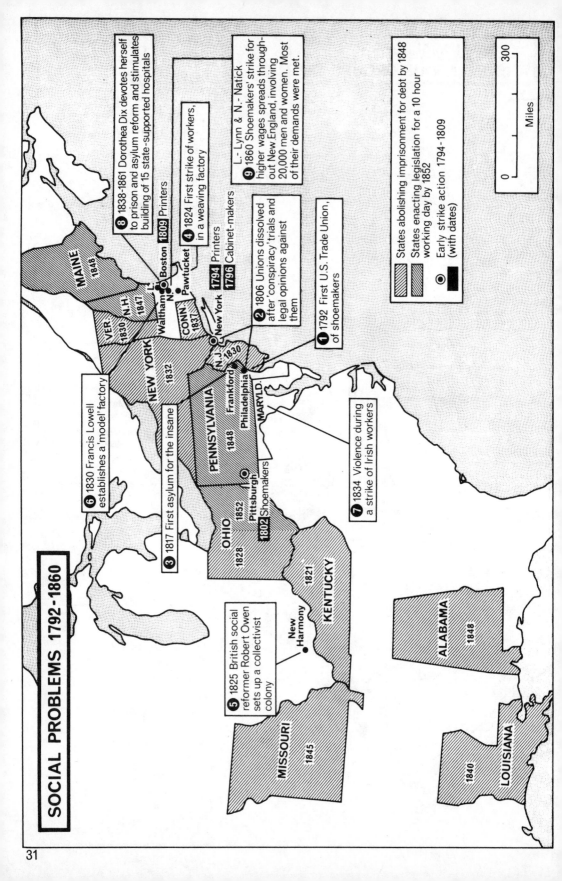

SOCIAL PROBLEMS 1792-1860

8 1838-1861 Dorothea Dix devotes herself to prison and asylum reform and stimulates building of 15 state-supported hospitals

1809 Printers

4 1824 First strike of workers, in a weaving factory

1794 Printers

1796 Cabinet-makers

L- Lynn & N.- Natick

9 1860 Shoemakers' strike for higher wages spreads throughout New England, involving 20,000 men and women. Most of their demands were met.

2 1806 Unions dissolved after 'conspiracy' trials and legal opinions against them

1 1792 First U.S. Trade Union, of shoemakers

6 1830 Francis Lowell establishes a 'model' factory

3 1817 First asylum for the insane

7 1834 Violence during a strike of Irish workers

5 1825 British social reformer Robert Owen sets up a collectivist colony

MAINE
1848

VER.
1830

N.H.
1847

Boston

Waltham
N.

Pawtucket

CONN.
1837

New York

NEW YORK
1832

N.J.
1830

Frankford

Philadelphia

PENNSYLVANIA
1848

MARYLD.

Pittsburgh
1852
1802 Shoemakers

OHIO
1828

KENTUCKY
1821

New Harmony

MISSOURI
1845

ALABAMA
1848

LOUISIANA
1840

States abolishing imprisonment for debt by 1848

States enacting legislation for a 10 hour working day by 1852

Early strike action 1794-1809 (with dates)

0   300
Miles

31

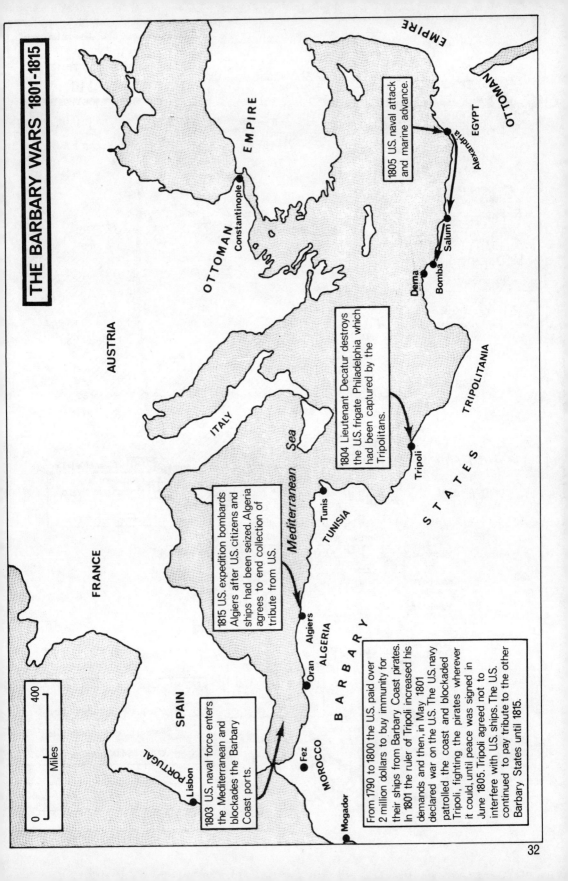

THE BARBARY WARS 1801-1815

OTTOMAN EMPIRE

OTTOMAN EMPIRE

1805 U.S. naval attack and marine advance.

Alexandria

EGYPT

Salum

Bomba

Derna

OTTOMAN EMPIRE

Constantinople

AUSTRIA

ITALY

Mediterranean Sea

1804 Lieutenant Decatur destroys the U.S. frigate Philadelphia which had been captured by the Tripolitans.

Tripoli

TRIPOLITANIA

B A R B A R Y   S T A T E S

FRANCE

1815 U.S. expedition bombards Algiers after U.S. citizens and ships had been seized. Algeria agrees to end collection of tribute from U.S.

Tunis

TUNISIA

Algiers

Oran

ALGERIA

SPAIN

PORTUGAL

Lisbon

Fez

MOROCCO

Mogador

1803 U.S. naval force enters the Mediterranean and blockades the Barbary Coast ports.

From 1790 to 1800 the U.S. paid over 2 million dollars to buy immunity for their ships from Barbary Coast pirates. In 1801 the ruler of Tripoli increased his demands and then, in May 1801 declared war on the U.S. The U.S. navy patrolled the coast and blockaded Tripoli, fighting the pirates wherever it could, until peace was signed in June 1805. Tripoli agreed not to interfere with U.S. ships. The U.S. continued to pay tribute to the other Barbary States until 1815.

0   Miles   400

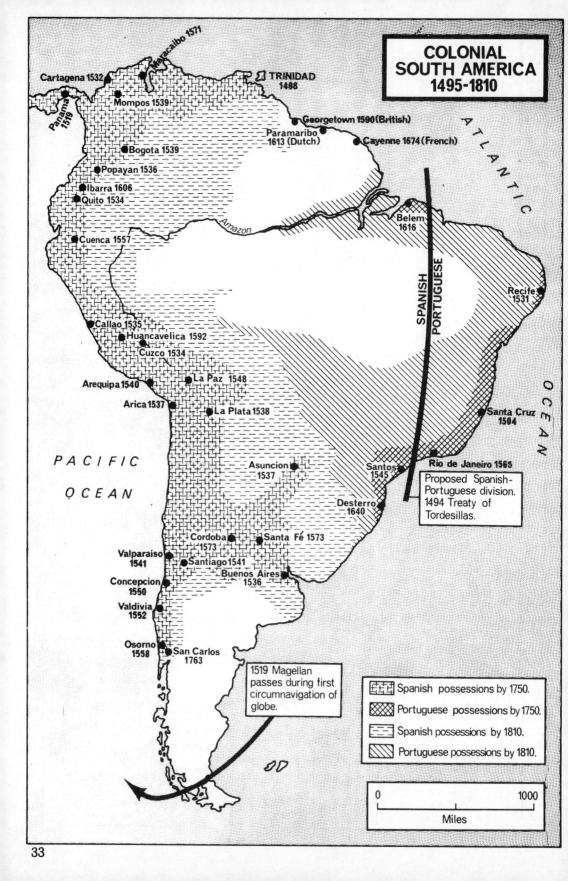

COLONIAL
SOUTH AMERICA
1495-1810

Maracaibo 1571

Cartagena 1532

Panama
1519

Mompos 1539

Georgetown 1590 (British)

Paramaribo
1613 (Dutch)

Cayenne 1674 (French)

Bogota 1539

Popayan 1536

Ibarra 1606
Quito 1534

Amazon

TRINIDAD
1498

ATLANTIC

Belem
1616

Cuenca 1557

SPANISH

PORTUGUESE

Recife
1531

Callao 1535
Huancavelica 1592
Cuzco 1534

La Paz 1548

Arequipa 1540

Arica 1537

La Plata 1538

Santa Cruz
1504

OCEAN

PACIFIC

OCEAN

Asuncion
1537

Santos
1545

Rio de Janeiro 1565

Desterro
1640

Proposed Spanish-
Portuguese division.
1494 Treaty of
Tordesillas.

Cordoba
1573

Santa Fé 1573

Valparaiso
1541

Santiago 1541

Buenos Aires
1536

Concepcion
1550

Valdivia
1552

Osorno
1558

San Carlos
1763

1519 Magellan
passes during first
circumnavigation of
globe.

Spanish possessions by 1750.

Portuguese possessions by 1750.

Spanish possessions by 1810.

Portuguese possessions by 1810.

0   1000

Miles

33

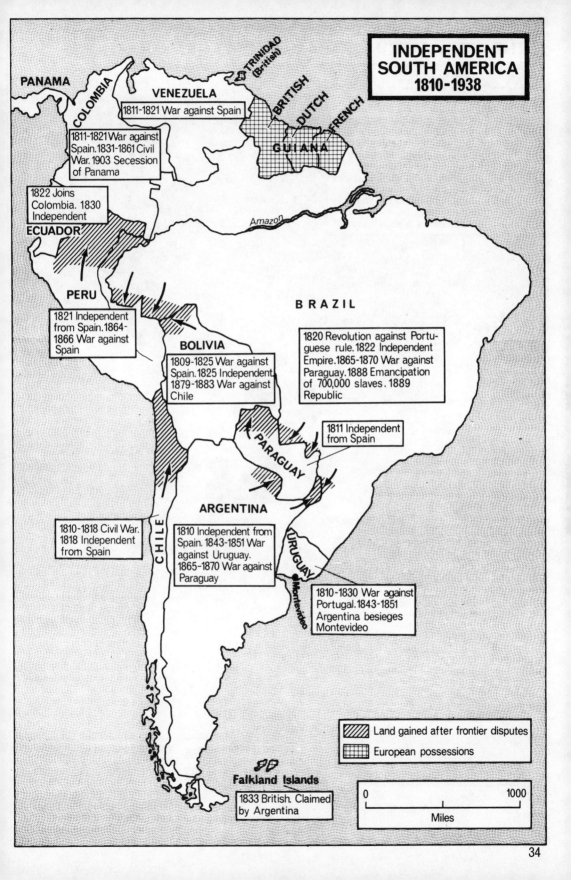

INDEPENDENT SOUTH AMERICA 1810-1938

PANAMA

COLOMBIA

VENEZUELA

1811-1821 War against Spain

1811-1821 War against Spain. 1831-1861 Civil War. 1903 Secession of Panama

1822 Joins Colombia. 1830 Independent

ECUADOR

TRINIDAD (British)

BRITISH

DUTCH

FRENCH

GUIANA

Amazon

BRAZIL

PERU

1821 Independent from Spain. 1864-1866 War against Spain

BOLIVIA

1809-1825 War against Spain. 1825 Independent. 1879-1883 War against Chile

1820 Revolution against Portuguese rule. 1822 Independent Empire. 1865-1870 War against Paraguay. 1888 Emancipation of 700,000 slaves. 1889 Republic

1811 Independent from Spain

PARAGUAY

ARGENTINA

CHILE

1810-1818 Civil War. 1818 Independent from Spain

1810 Independent from Spain. 1843-1851 War against Uruguay. 1865-1870 War against Paraguay

URUGUAY

Montevideo

1810-1830 War against Portugal. 1843-1851 Argentina besieges Montevideo

/// Land gained after frontier disputes

▦ European possessions

Falkland Islands

1833 British. Claimed by Argentina

0   1000

Miles

34

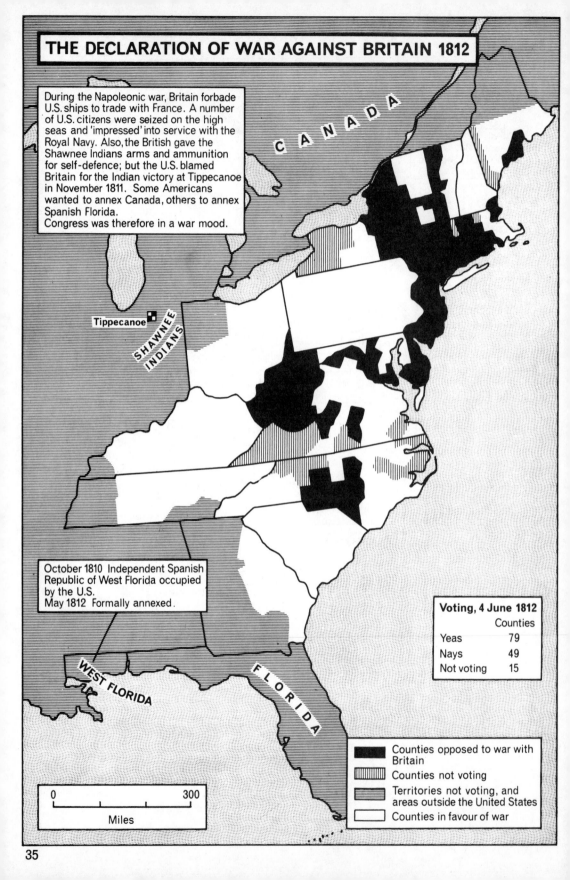

THE DECLARATION OF WAR AGAINST BRITAIN 1812

During the Napoleonic war, Britain forbade U.S. ships to trade with France. A number of U.S. citizens were seized on the high seas and 'impressed' into service with the Royal Navy. Also, the British gave the Shawnee Indians arms and ammunition for self-defence; but the U.S. blamed Britain for the Indian victory at Tippecanoe in November 1811. Some Americans wanted to annex Canada, others to annex Spanish Florida.
Congress was therefore in a war mood.

CANADA

Tippecanoe

SHAWNEE INDIANS

October 1810 Independent Spanish Republic of West Florida occupied by the U.S.
May 1812 Formally annexed.

WEST FLORIDA

FLORIDA

Voting, 4 June 1812

	Counties
Yeas	79
Nays	49
Not voting	15

Counties opposed to war with Britain

Counties not voting

Territories not voting, and areas outside the United States

Counties in favour of war

| 0 | 300 |
Miles

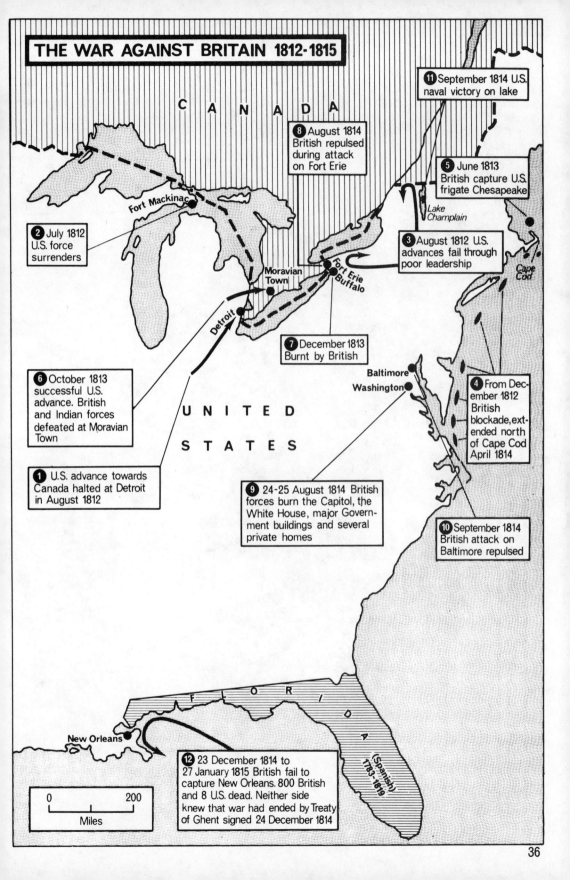

THE WAR AGAINST BRITAIN 1812-1815

C A N A D A

11 September 1814 U.S. naval victory on lake

8 August 1814 British repulsed during attack on Fort Erie

5 June 1813 British capture U.S. frigate Chesapeake

Fort Mackinac

Lake Champlain

2 July 1812 U.S. force surrenders

Cape Cod

Moravian Town

Fort Erie
Buffalo

3 August 1812 U.S. advances fail through poor leadership

Detroit

6 October 1813 successful U.S. advance. British and Indian forces defeated at Moravian Town

7 December 1813 Burnt by British

Baltimore

Washington

4 From December 1812 British blockade, extended north of Cape Cod April 1814

U N I T E D

S T A T E S

1 U.S. advance towards Canada halted at Detroit in August 1812

9 24-25 August 1814 British forces burn the Capitol, the White House, major Government buildings and several private homes

10 September 1814 British attack on Baltimore repulsed

F L O R I D A

New Orleans

(Spanish) 1783-1819

12 23 December 1814 to 27 January 1815 British fail to capture New Orleans. 800 British and 8 U.S. dead. Neither side knew that war had ended by Treaty of Ghent signed 24 December 1814

0   200
Miles

36

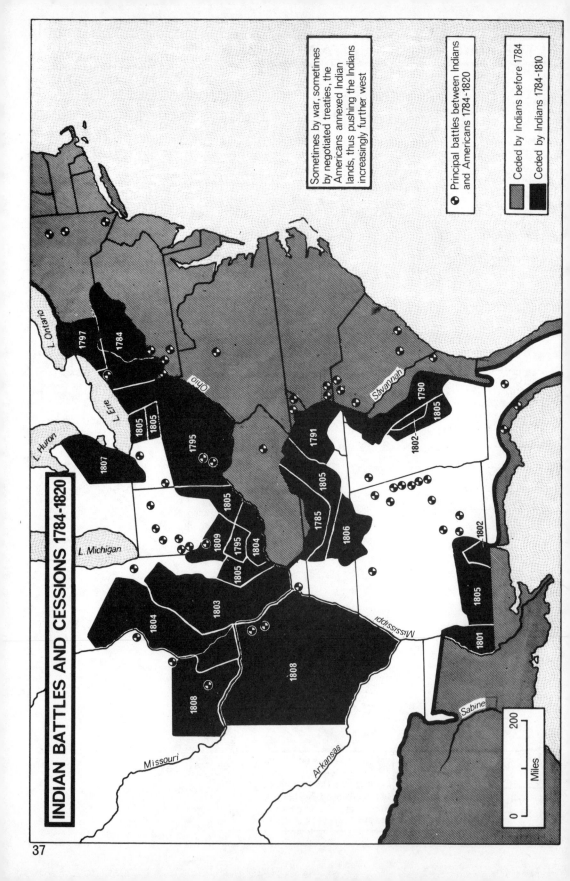

INDIAN BATTLES AND CESSIONS 1784-1820

Sometimes by war, sometimes by negotiated treaties, the Americans annexed Indian lands, thus pushing the Indians increasingly further west

- ● Principal battles between Indians and Americans 1784-1820
- Ceded by Indians before 1784
- Ceded by Indians 1784-1810

L. Ontario

L. Erie

L. Huron

L. Michigan

Ohio

Savannah

Mississippi

Missouri

Arkansas

Sabine

1797
1784
1805
1805
1807
1795
1805
1809
1795
1804
1805
1803
1804
1808
1808
1791
1805
1785
1806
1790
1805
1802
1802
1805
1801

0   200
Miles

37

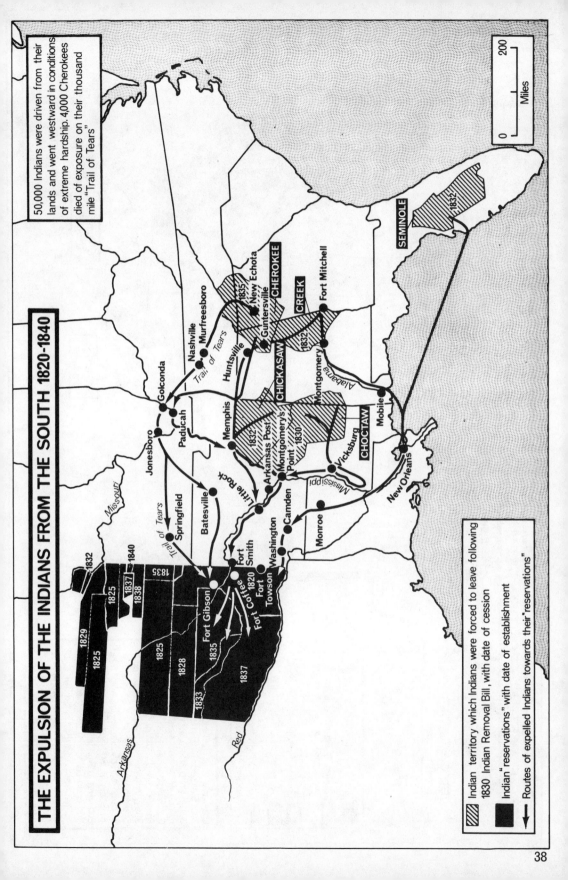

THE EXPULSION OF THE INDIANS FROM THE SOUTH 1820-1840

50,000 Indians were driven from their lands and went westward in conditions of extreme hardship. 4,000 Cherokees died of exposure on their thousand mile "Trail of Tears"

SEMINOLE

1832

CHEROKEE

CREEK

CHICKASAW

CHOCTAW

1835 New Echota
Guntersville
Fort Mitchell
1832
Montgomery
Mobile
Vicksburg

Murfreesboro
Nashville
Huntsville
Trail of Tears
Golconda
Paducah
Memphis
Jonesboro
1832 Arkansas Post
Montgomery's Point 1830
New Orleans
Monroe
Camden
Washington
Fort Towson
Fort Coffee 1820
Fort Smith
Little Rock
Batesville
Springfield
Trail of Tears
1835 Fort Gibson
1825
1828
1833
1837
1835
Red
Arkansas
Missouri
Alabama
Mississippi

1832
1840
1837
1838
1829
1825
1825

0   200
Miles

Indian territory which Indians were forced to leave following 1830 Indian Removal Bill, with date of cession

Indian "reservations" with date of establishment

Routes of expelled Indians towards their "reservations"

38

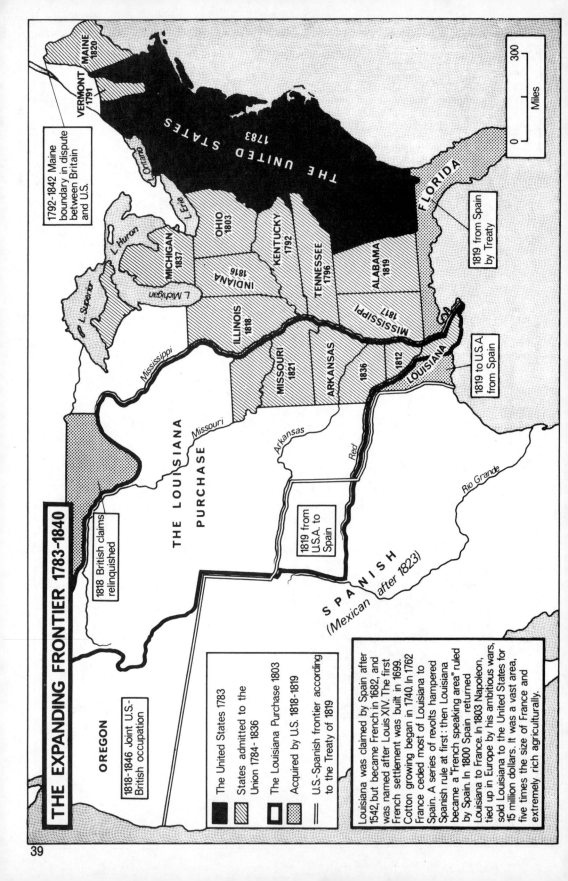

THE EXPANDING FRONTIER 1783-1840

THE UNITED STATES 1783

THE LOUISIANA PURCHASE

S P A N I S H
(Mexican after 1823)

OREGON

1818-1846 Joint U.S.-British occupation

1818 British claims relinquished

1792-1842 Maine boundary in dispute between Britain and U.S.

1819 from Spain by Treaty

1819 to U.S.A. from Spain

1819 from U.S.A. to Spain

States and dates

MAINE 1820
VERMONT 1791
MICHIGAN 1837
OHIO 1803
INDIANA 1816
ILLINOIS 1818
KENTUCKY 1792
TENNESSEE 1796
MISSISSIPPI 1817
ALABAMA 1819
MISSOURI 1821
ARKANSAS 1836
LOUISIANA 1812
FLORIDA

Rivers and Lakes
Mississippi, Missouri, Arkansas, Red, Rio Grande, L. Superior, L. Huron, L. Michigan, L. Erie, L. Ontario

Scale
0 — 300 Miles

Legend

- ■ The United States 1783
- ▨ States admitted to the Union 1784-1836
- □ The Louisiana Purchase 1803
- ▦ Acquired by U.S. 1818-1819
- ═ U.S.-Spanish frontier according to the Treaty of 1819

Louisiana was claimed by Spain after 1542, but became French in 1682, and was named after Louis XIV. The first French settlement was built in 1699. Cotton growing began in 1740. In 1762 France ceded most of Louisiana to Spain. A series of revolts hampered Spanish rule at first: then Louisiana became a "French speaking area" ruled by Spain. In 1800 Spain returned Louisiana to France. In 1803 Napoleon, tied up in Europe by his ambitious wars, sold Louisiana to the United States for 15 million dollars. It was a vast area, five times the size of France and extremely rich agriculturally.

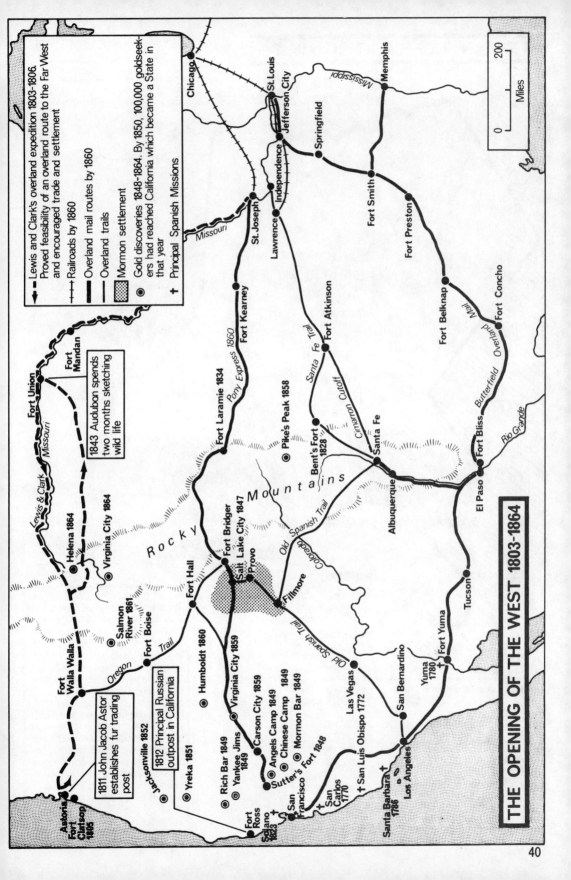

THE OPENING OF THE WEST 1803-1864

Legend (inset box):

- Lewis and Clark's overland expedition 1803-1806. Proved feasibility of an overland route to the Far West and encouraged trade and settlement
- ┼┼┼ Railroads by 1860
- ▬ Overland mail routes by 1860
- Overland trails
- ░ Mormon settlement
- ◉ Gold discoveries 1848-1864. By 1850, 100,000 goldseekers had reached California which became a State in that year
- ✝ Principal Spanish Missions

1843 Audubon spends two months sketching wild life

1811 John Jacob Astor establishes fur trading post

1812 Principal Russian outpost in California

Chicago
St. Louis
Jefferson City
Memphis
Springfield
Independence
Lawrence
Fort Smith
St. Joseph
Fort Preston
Missouri
Fort Concho
Fort Belknap
Fort Mandan
Fort Union
Fort Kearney
Fort Atkinson
Lewis & Clark
Missouri
Helena 1864
Virginia City 1864
Fort Laramie 1834
Pony Express 1860
Pike's Peak 1858
Bent's Fort 1828
Santa Fe
Santa Fe Trail
Cimarron Cutoff
Fort Bliss
El Paso
Rio Grande
Butterfield Overland Mail
Fort Walla Walla
Salmon River 1861
Fort Boise
Rocky Mountains
Fort Hall
Fort Bridger
Salt Lake City 1847
Provo
Fillmore
Old Spanish Trail
Colorado
Albuquerque
Jacksonville 1852
Oregon Trail
Humboldt 1860
Virginia City 1859
Carson City 1859
Angels Camp 1849
Chinese Camp 1849
Mormon Bar 1849
Yreka 1851
Rich Bar 1849
Yankee Jims 1849
Sutter's Fort 1848
Fort Ross
Las Vegas
San Bernardino
Tucson
Yuma 1780
Fort Yuma
Old Spanish Trail
San Luis Obispo 1772
San Carlos 1770
San Francisco
Solano 1823
San Luis Obispo
Santa Barbara 1786
Los Angeles

0   200
Miles

Astoria
Fort Clatsop 1805

40

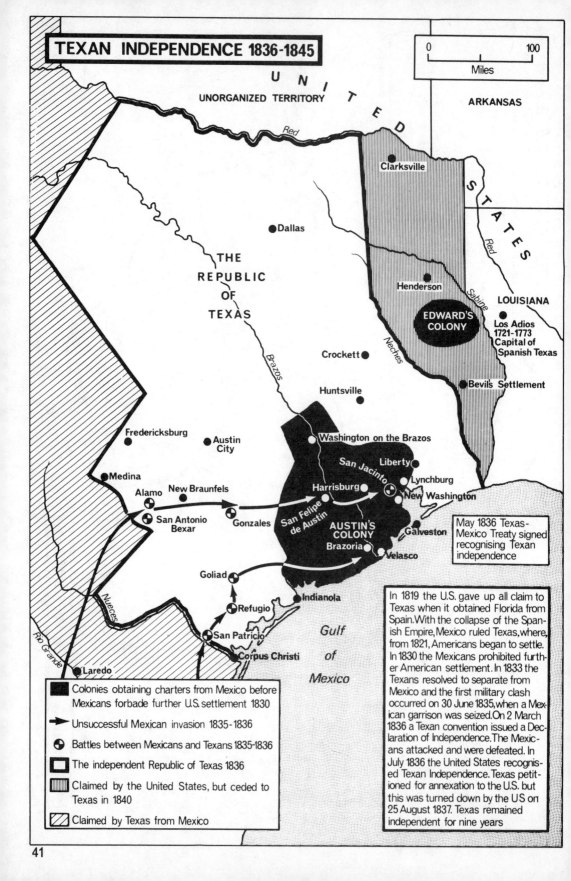

TEXAN INDEPENDENCE 1836-1845

0 ——— 100
Miles

U N I T E D

UNORGANIZED TERRITORY

ARKANSAS

S T A T E S

Red

Clarksville

THE
REPUBLIC
OF
TEXAS

Dallas

Henderson

LOUISIANA

Neches

EDWARD'S
COLONY

Los Adios
1721-1773
Capital of
Spanish Texas

Crockett

Bevils Settlement

Brazos

Huntsville

Fredericksburg

Austin
City

Washington on the Brazos

Liberty

San Jacinto

Lynchburg

Medina

Harrisburg

New Washington

Alamo

New Braunfels

San Felipe
de Austin

May 1836 Texas-
Mexico Treaty signed
recognising Texan
independence

San Antonio
Bexar

Gonzales

AUSTIN'S
COLONY

Galveston

Brazoria

Velasco

Goliad

Indianola

Gulf

Refugio

of

San Patricio

Mexico

Rio Grande

Nueces

Corpus Christi

Laredo

■ Colonies obtaining charters from Mexico before
Mexicans forbade further U.S. settlement 1830

➔ Unsuccessful Mexican invasion 1835-1836

✛ Battles between Mexicans and Texans 1835-1836

☐ The independent Republic of Texas 1836

▥ Claimed by the United States, but ceded to
Texas in 1840

▨ Claimed by Texas from Mexico

In 1819 the U.S. gave up all claim to
Texas when it obtained Florida from
Spain. With the collapse of the Spanish Empire, Mexico ruled Texas, where,
from 1821, Americans began to settle.
In 1830 the Mexicans prohibited further American settlement. In 1833 the
Texans resolved to separate from
Mexico and the first military clash
occurred on 30 June 1835, when a Mexican garrison was seized. On 2 March
1836 a Texan convention issued a Declaration of Independence. The Mexicans attacked and were defeated. In
July 1836 the United States recognised Texan Independence. Texas petit-
ioned for annexation to the U.S. but
this was turned down by the US on
25 August 1837. Texas remained
independent for nine years

41

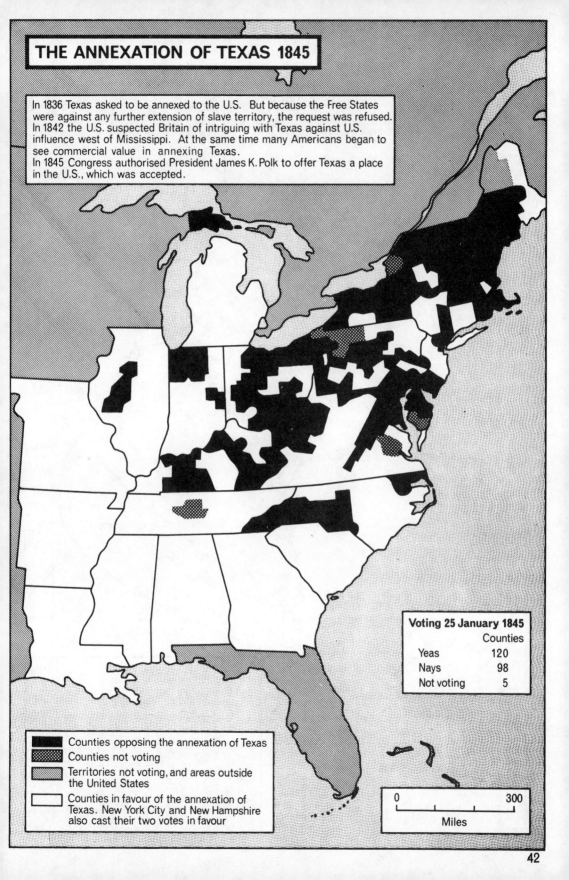

THE ANNEXATION OF TEXAS 1845

In 1836 Texas asked to be annexed to the U.S. But because the Free States were against any further extension of slave territory, the request was refused. In 1842 the U.S. suspected Britain of intriguing with Texas against U.S. influence west of Mississippi. At the same time many Americans began to see commercial value in annexing Texas.
In 1845 Congress authorised President James K. Polk to offer Texas a place in the U.S., which was accepted.

Voting 25 January 1845

	Counties
Yeas	120
Nays	98
Not voting	5

Counties opposing the annexation of Texas

Counties not voting

Territories not voting, and areas outside the United States

Counties in favour of the annexation of Texas. New York City and New Hampshire also cast their two votes in favour

0   300

Miles

THE WAR AGAINST MEXICO 1846-1848

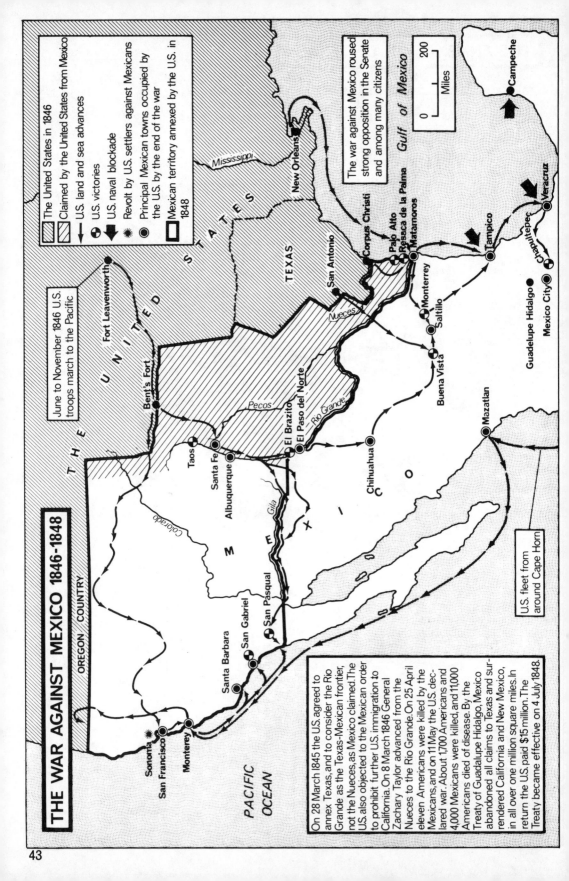

Legend:

- ▨ The United States in 1846
- ▧ Claimed by the United States from Mexico
- ↓ U.S. land and sea advances
- ⊕ U.S. victories
- ⬇ U.S. naval blockade
- ✳ Revolt by U.S. settlers against Mexicans
- ◉ Principal Mexican towns occupied by the U.S. by the end of the war
- ▢ Mexican territory annexed by the U.S. in 1848

June to November 1846 U.S. troops march to the Pacific

The war against Mexico roused strong opposition in the Senate and among many citizens

Gulf of Mexico

0   200
Miles

THE UNITED STATES

OREGON COUNTRY

PACIFIC OCEAN

MEXICO

Mississippi

New Orleans

TEXAS

San Antonio

Nueces

Corpus Christi

Palo Alto
Resaca de la Palma
Matamoros

Monterrey

Saltillo

Buena Vista

Tampico

Chapultepec
Veracruz

Guadalupe Hidalgo

Mexico City

Campeche

Fort Leavenworth

Bent's Fort

Pecos

El Brazito
El Paso del Norte

Rio Grande

Chihuahua

Mazatlan

Taos

Santa Fe

Albuquerque

Gila

Colorado

San Pasqual

San Gabriel

Santa Barbara

Monterrey

San Francisco

Sonoma

U.S. fleet from around Cape Horn

On 28 March 1845 the U.S. agreed to annex Texas, and to consider the Rio Grande as the Texas-Mexican frontier, not the Nueces, as Mexico claimed. The U.S. also objected to the Mexican order to prohibit further U.S. immigration to California. On 8 March 1846 General Zachary Taylor advanced from the Nueces to the Rio Grande. On 25 April eleven Americans were killed by the Mexicans, and on 11 May the U.S. declared war. About 1,700 Americans and 4,000 Mexicans were killed, and 11,000 Americans died of disease. By the Treaty of Guadalupe Hidalgo, Mexico abandoned all claims to Texas and surrendered California and New Mexico, in all over one million square miles. In return the U.S. paid $15 million. The Treaty became effective on 4 July 1848.

43

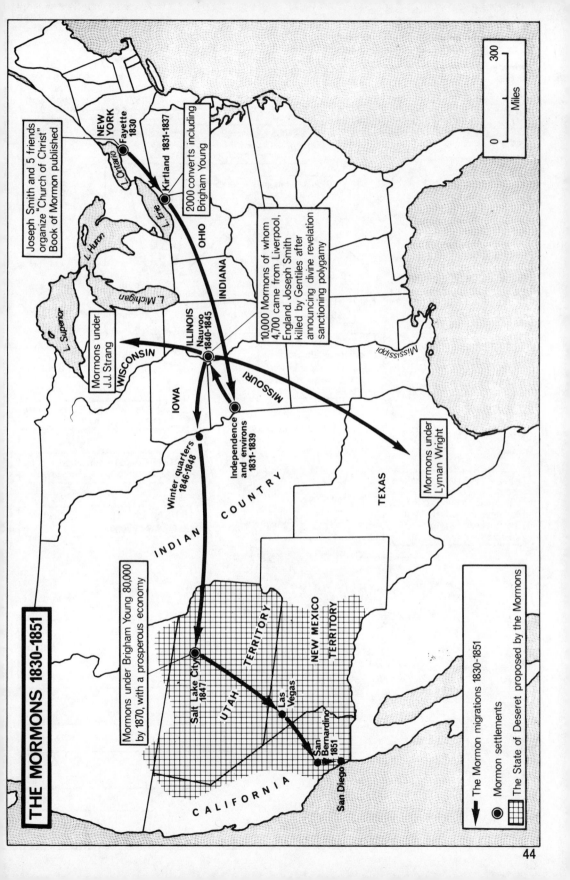

THE MORMONS 1830-1851

Joseph Smith and 5 friends organize "Church of Christ" Book of Mormon published

NEW YORK
Fayette 1830

Kirtland 1831-1837

2000 converts including Brigham Young

OHIO

INDIANA

L. Huron

L. Michigan

L. Superior

L. Ontario

L. Erie

Mormons under J. J. Strang

WISCONSIN

ILLINOIS
Nauvoo 1840-1845

10,000 Mormons of whom 4,700 came from Liverpool, England. Joseph Smith killed by Gentiles after announcing divine revelation sanctioning polygamy

Mississippi

IOWA

MISSOURI

Winter quarters 1846-1848

Independence and environs 1831-1839

INDIAN COUNTRY

TEXAS

Mormons under Lyman Wright

Mormons under Brigham Young 80,000 by 1870, with a prosperous economy

Salt Lake City 1847–

UTAH TERRITORY

NEW MEXICO TERRITORY

Las Vegas

San Bernardino 1851

San Diego

CALIFORNIA

Miles
0   300

The Mormon migrations 1830-1851

● Mormon settlements

The State of Deseret proposed by the Mormons

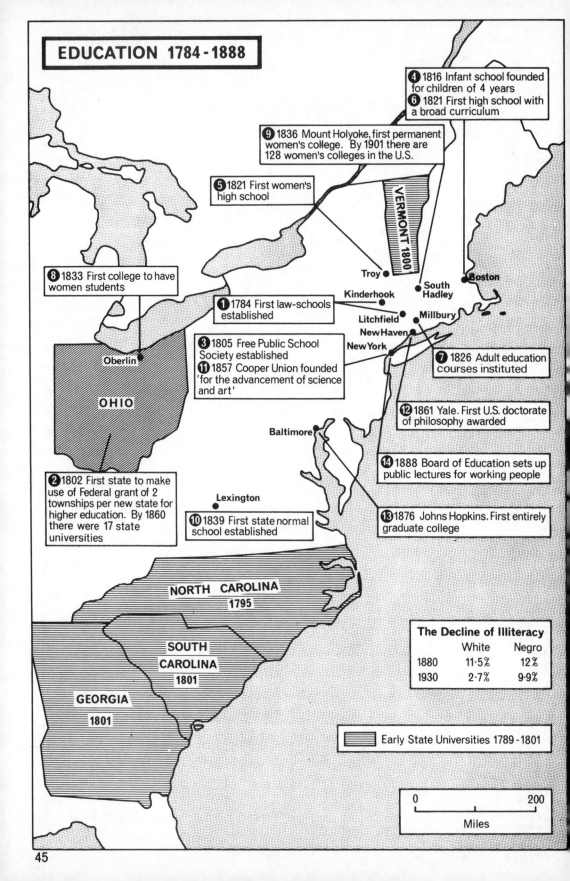

EDUCATION 1784-1888

4 1816 Infant school founded for children of 4 years

6 1821 First high school with a broad curriculum

9 1836 Mount Holyoke, first permanent women's college. By 1901 there are 128 women's colleges in the U.S.

5 1821 First women's high school

VERMONT 1800

8 1833 First college to have women students

Troy

Kinderhook

South Hadley

Boston

1 1784 First law-schools established

Litchfield

Millbury

New Haven

New York

3 1805 Free Public School Society established

11 1857 Cooper Union founded 'for the advancement of science and art'

Oberlin

OHIO

7 1826 Adult education courses instituted

12 1861 Yale. First U.S. doctorate of philosophy awarded

Baltimore

14 1888 Board of Education sets up public lectures for working people

2 1802 First state to make use of Federal grant of 2 townships per new state for higher education. By 1860 there were 17 state universities

Lexington

10 1839 First state normal school established

13 1876 Johns Hopkins. First entirely graduate college

NORTH CAROLINA 1795

SOUTH CAROLINA 1801

The Decline of Illiteracy		
	White	Negro
1880	11·5%	12%
1930	2·7%	9·9%

GEORGIA 1801

Early State Universities 1789-1801

0		200
Miles		

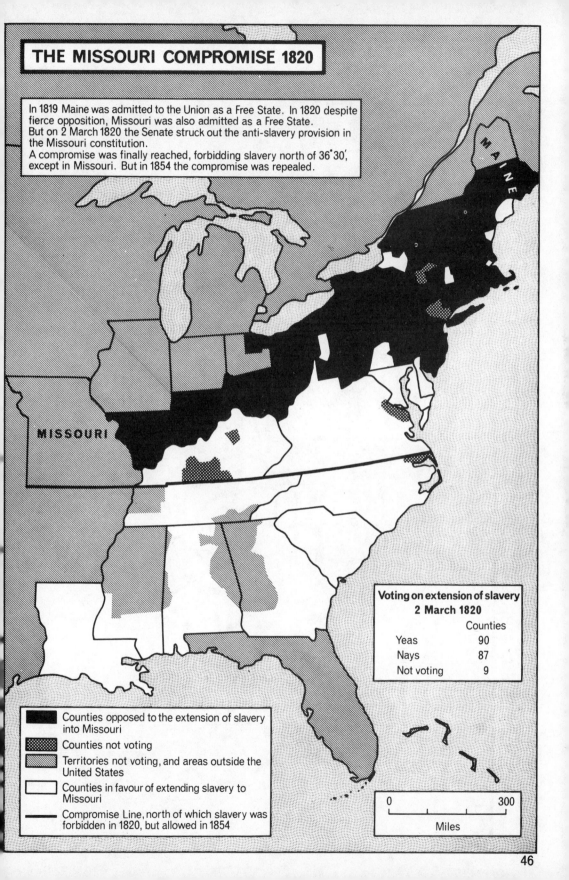

THE MISSOURI COMPROMISE 1820

In 1819 Maine was admitted to the Union as a Free State. In 1820 despite fierce opposition, Missouri was also admitted as a Free State.
But on 2 March 1820 the Senate struck out the anti-slavery provision in the Missouri constitution.
A compromise was finally reached, forbidding slavery north of 36°30′, except in Missouri. But in 1854 the compromise was repealed.

MAINE

MISSOURI

Voting on extension of slavery
2 March 1820

	Counties
Yeas	90
Nays	87
Not voting	9

■ Counties opposed to the extension of slavery into Missouri

▨ Counties not voting

▨ Territories not voting, and areas outside the United States

□ Counties in favour of extending slavery to Missouri

— Compromise Line, north of which slavery was forbidden in 1820, but allowed in 1854

0   300

Miles

46

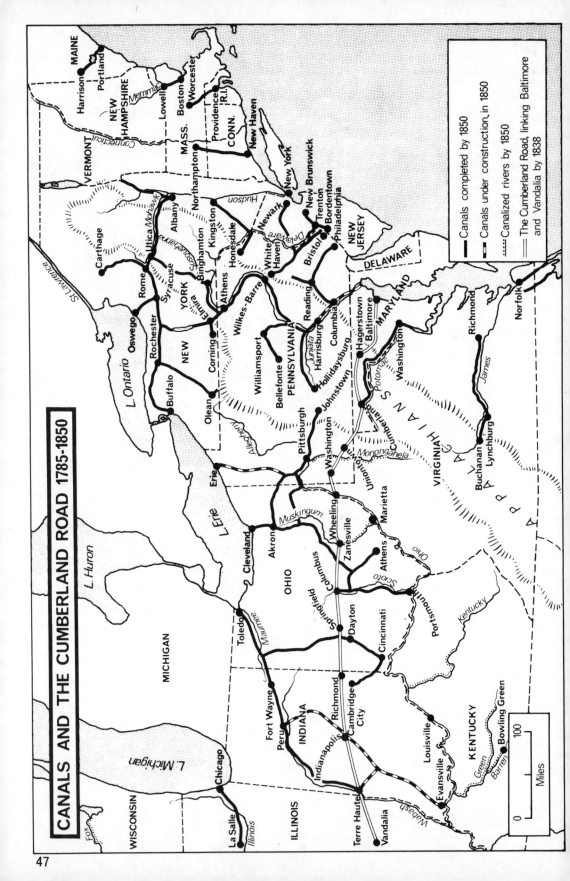

CANALS AND THE CUMBERLAND ROAD 1785-1850

Legend:
- Canals completed by 1850
- Canals under construction, in 1850
- Canalized rivers by 1850
- The Cumberland Road, linking Baltimore and Vandalia by 1838

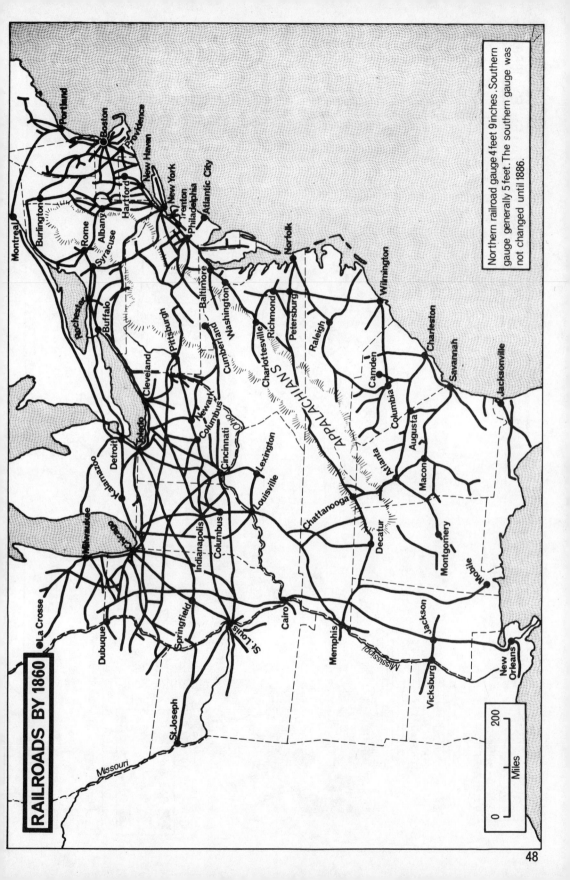

RAILROADS BY 1860

Northern railroad gauge 4 feet 9 inches. Southern gauge generally 5 feet. The southern gauge was not changed until 1886.

0   200
Miles

48

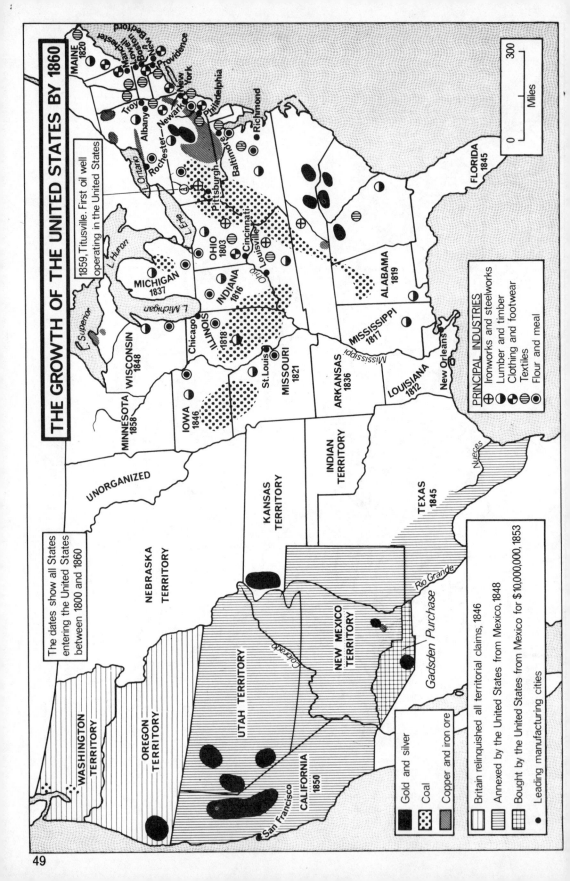

THE GROWTH OF THE UNITED STATES BY 1860

1859, Titusville. First oil well operating in the United States

The dates show all States entering the United States between 1800 and 1860

PRINCIPAL INDUSTRIES
- Ironworks and steelworks
- Lumber and timber
- Clothing and footwear
- Textiles
- Flour and meal

MAINE 1820

New Bedford
Providence
New York
Troy
Albany
Newark
Philadelphia
Rochester
Pittsburgh
Baltimore
Richmond

L. Ontario
L. Erie
L. Huron
L. Michigan
L. Superior

MICHIGAN 1837

OHIO 1803
Cincinnati
Louisville

INDIANA 1816

ILLINOIS 1818
Chicago

WISCONSIN 1848

MINNESOTA 1858

IOWA 1846

MISSOURI 1821
St. Louis

ALABAMA 1819

MISSISSIPPI 1817

ARKANSAS 1836

LOUISIANA 1812
New Orleans

FLORIDA 1845

UNORGANIZED

NEBRASKA TERRITORY

KANSAS TERRITORY

INDIAN TERRITORY

TEXAS 1845

WASHINGTON TERRITORY

OREGON TERRITORY

UTAH TERRITORY

NEW MEXICO TERRITORY

CALIFORNIA 1850
San Francisco

Rio Grande
Gadsden Purchase
Nueces
Colorado
Mississippi

- Gold and silver
- Coal
- Copper and iron ore

- Britain relinquished all territorial claims, 1846
- Annexed by the United States from Mexico, 1848
- Bought by the United States from Mexico for $10,000,000, 1853
- Leading manufacturing cities

0   300
Miles

49

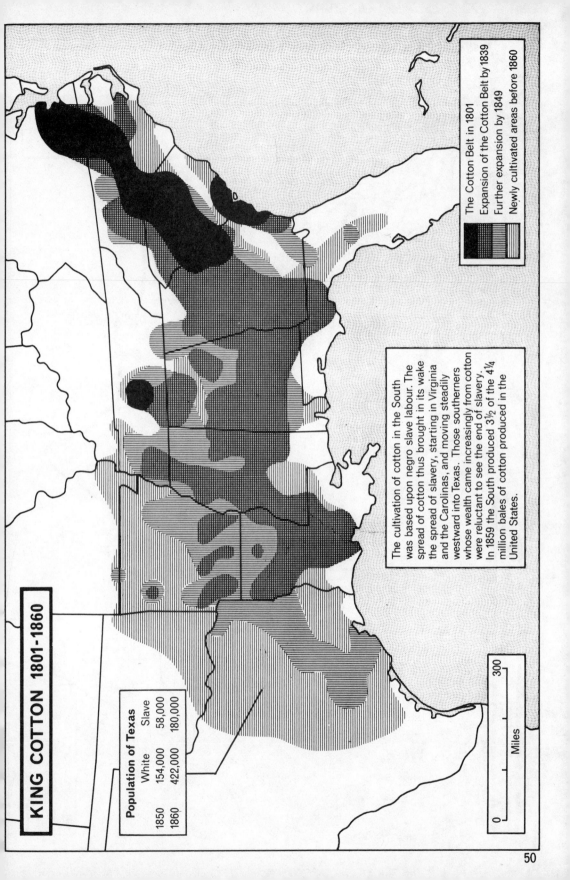

KING COTTON 1801-1860

Population of Texas

	White	Slave
1850	154,000	58,000
1860	422,000	180,000

The Cotton Belt in 1801
Expansion of the Cotton Belt by 1839
Further expansion by 1849
Newly cultivated areas before 1860

The cultivation of cotton in the South was based upon negro slave labour. The spread of cotton thus brought in its wake the spread of slavery, starting in Virginia and the Carolinas, and moving steadily westward into Texas. Those southerners whose wealth came increasingly from cotton were reluctant to see the end of slavery. In 1859 the South produced 3½ of the 4¼ million bales of cotton produced in the United States.

0 — 300 Miles

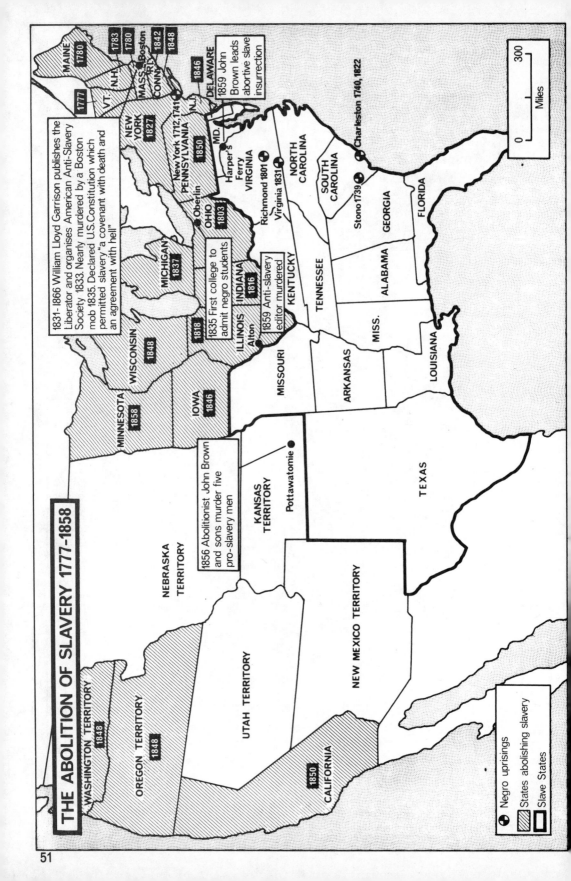

THE ABOLITION OF SLAVERY 1777-1858

1831- 1866 William Lloyd Garrison publishes the Liberator and organises American Anti-Slavery Society 1833. Nearly murdered by a Boston mob 1835. Declared U.S.Constitution which permitted slavery "a covenant with death and an agreement with hell"

1835 First college to admit negro students

1859 Anti-slavery editor murdered

1856 Abolitionist John Brown and sons murder five pro-slavery men

1859 John Brown leads abortive slave insurrection

300

0

Miles

MAINE 1780

1783 1780 1842 1848

N.H.

VT. 1777

MASS. Boston

CONN. 1848

DELAWARE 1846

NEW YORK 1827

New York 1712,1741

N.J. 1820

PENNSYLVANIA 1850

MD.

Harper's Ferry

Oberlin

OHIO 1803

Richmond 1801

VIRGINIA

Virginia 1831

NORTH CAROLINA

Charleston 1740, 1822

SOUTH CAROLINA

Stono 1739

GEORGIA

FLORIDA

MICHIGAN 1837

INDIANA 1816

ILLINOIS 1818

Alton

KENTUCKY

TENNESSEE

WISCONSIN 1848

IOWA 1846

MISSOURI

ARKANSAS

MISS.

ALABAMA

LOUISIANA

MINNESOTA 1858

KANSAS TERRITORY

Pottawatomie

NEBRASKA TERRITORY

TEXAS

WASHINGTON TERRITORY 1848

OREGON TERRITORY 1848

UTAH TERRITORY

NEW MEXICO TERRITORY

CALIFORNIA 1850

Negro uprisings

States abolishing slavery

Slave States

51

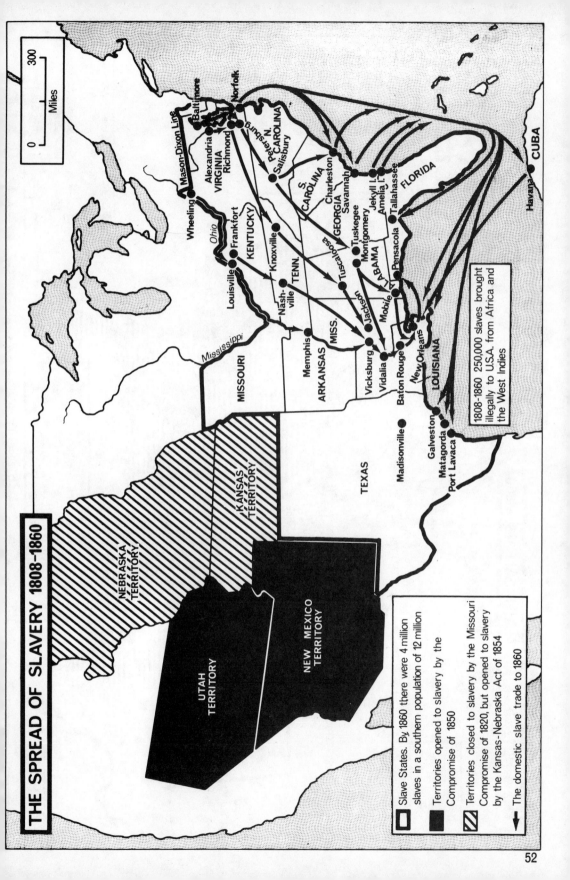

THE SPREAD OF SLAVERY 1808–1860

0   300

Miles

Mason-Dixon Line

Baltimore
Norfolk
Alexandria
VIRGINIA
Richmond
Wheeling
Peters N.
Salisbury
N. CAROLINA
S. CAROLINA
Charleston
Savannah
GEORGIA
Jekyll I.
Amelia I.
Tallahassee
FLORIDA
Pensacola
Tuskegee
Montgomery
ALABAMA
Ohio
Frankfort
KENTUCKY
Knoxville
Louisville
Nashville
TENN.
Tuscaloosa
Jackson
Mobile
Vicksburg
Vidalia
Baton Rouge
New Orleans
LOUISIANA
Memphis
ARKANSAS
MISS.
Mississippi
MISSOURI
Galveston
Matagorda
Port Lavaca
Madisonville
TEXAS
KANSAS TERRITORY
NEBRASKA TERRITORY
UTAH TERRITORY
NEW MEXICO TERRITORY
CUBA
Havana

1808–1860 250,000 slaves brought illegally to U.S.A. from Africa and the West Indies

☐ Slave States. By 1860 there were 4 million slaves in a southern population of 12 million

■ Territories opened to slavery by the Compromise of 1850

▨ Territories closed to slavery by the Missouri Compromise of 1820, but opened to slavery by the Kansas-Nebraska Act of 1854

→ The domestic slave trade to 1860

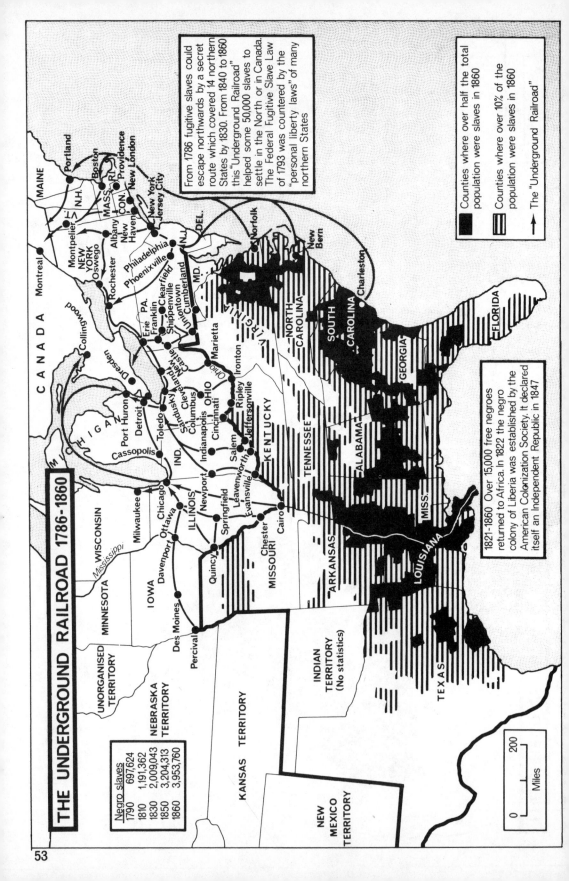

THE UNDERGROUND RAILROAD 1786-1860

From 1786 fugitive slaves could escape northwards by a secret route which covered 14 northern States by 1830. From 1840 to 1860 this "Underground Railroad" helped some 50,000 slaves to settle in the North or in Canada. The Federal Fugitive Slave Law of 1793 was countered by the "personal liberty laws" of many northern States

■	Counties where over half the total population were slaves in 1860
⦀	Counties where over 10% of the population were slaves in 1860
→	The "Underground Railroad"

1821-1860 Over 15,000 free negroes returned to Africa. In 1822 the negro colony of Liberia was established by the American Colonization Society. It declared itself an Independent Republic in 1847

Negro slaves
1790 697,624
1810 1,191,362
1830 2,009,043
1850 3,204,313
1860 3,953,760

0   200
Miles

53

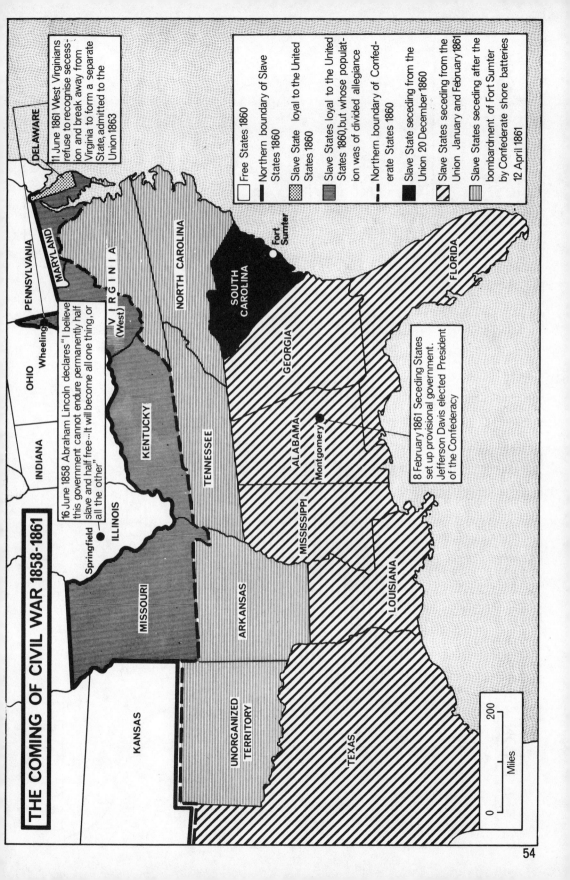

THE COMING OF CIVIL WAR 1858-1861

11 June 1861 West Virginians refuse to recognise secession and break away from Virginia to form a separate State, admitted to the Union 1863

16 June 1858 Abraham Lincoln declares "I believe this government cannot endure permanently half slave and half free...It will become all one thing, or all the other"

8 February 1861 Seceding States set up provisional government. Jefferson Davis elected President of the Confederacy

☐ Free States 1860

▌ Northern boundary of Slave States 1860

▒ Slave State loyal to the United States 1860

▤ Slave States loyal to the United States 1860, but whose population was of divided allegiance

■ Northern boundary of Confederate States 1860

▨ Slave State seceding from the Union 20 December 1860

▨ Slave States seceding from the Union January and February 1861

▥ Slave States seceding after the bombardment of Fort Sumter by Confederate shore batteries 12 April 1861

DELAWARE

MARYLAND

PENNSYLVANIA

Wheeling

OHIO

INDIANA

ILLINOIS

Springfield

MISSOURI

KANSAS

UNORGANIZED TERRITORY

VIRGINIA

VIRGINIA (West)

KENTUCKY

TENNESSEE

ARKANSAS

TEXAS

LOUISIANA

MISSISSIPPI

ALABAMA

Montgomery

GEORGIA

FLORIDA

NORTH CAROLINA

SOUTH CAROLINA

Fort Sumter

0   200

Miles

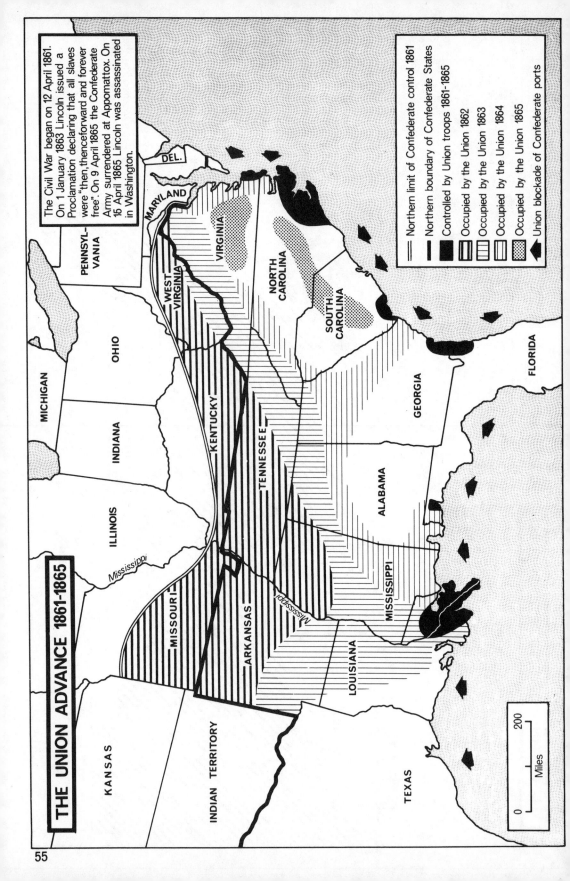

THE UNION ADVANCE 1861-1865

The Civil War began on 12 April 1861. On 1 January 1863 Lincoln issued a Proclamation declaring that all slaves were "then, thenceforward and forever free". On 9 April 1865 the Confederate Army surrendered at Appomattox. On 15 April 1865 Lincoln was assassinated in Washington.

Northern limit of Confederate control 1861

Northern boundary of Confederate States

Controlled by Union troops 1861-1865

Occupied by the Union 1862

Occupied by the Union 1863

Occupied by the Union 1864

Occupied by the Union 1865

Union blockade of Confederate ports

MICHIGAN

PENNSYLVANIA

DEL.

MARYLAND

WEST VIRGINIA

VIRGINIA

OHIO

INDIANA

ILLINOIS

NORTH CAROLINA

SOUTH CAROLINA

KENTUCKY

TENNESSEE

GEORGIA

ALABAMA

MISSISSIPPI

Mississippi

MISSOURI

ARKANSAS

Mississippi

LOUISIANA

FLORIDA

KANSAS

INDIAN TERRITORY

TEXAS

0   200

Miles

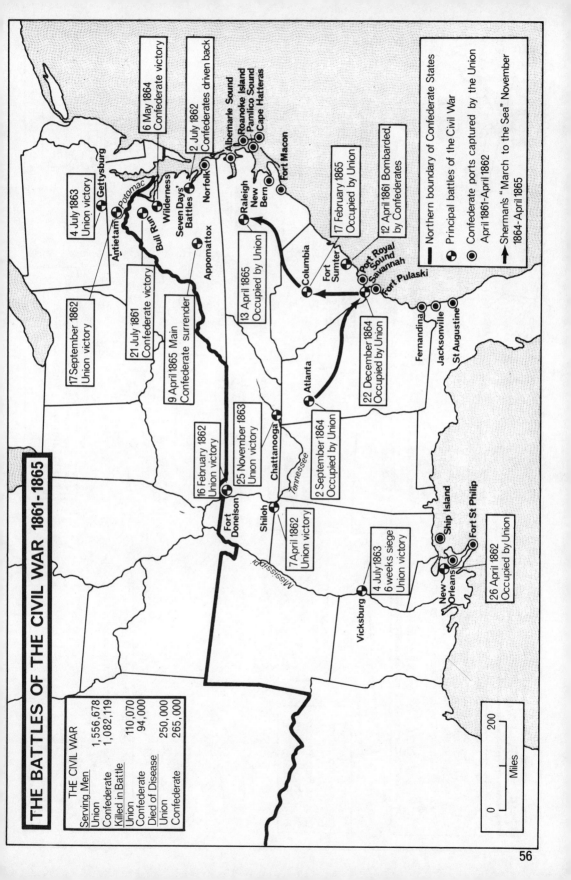

THE BATTLES OF THE CIVIL WAR 1861-1865

THE CIVIL WAR

Serving Men	
Union	1,556,678
Confederate	1,082,119
Killed in Battle	
Union	110,070
Confederate	94,000
Died of Disease	
Union	250,000
Confederate	265,000

Legend:
— Northern boundary of Confederate States
◉ Principal battles of the Civil War
◎ Confederate ports captured by the Union April 1861–April 1862
→ Sherman's "March to the Sea" November 1864–April 1865

Gettysburg — 4 July 1863 Union victory

6 May 1864 Confederate victory

2 July 1862 Confederates driven back

Albemarle Sound
Roanoke Island
Pamlico Sound
Cape Hatteras
Fort Macon

17 February 1865 Occupied by Union

12 April 1861 Bombarded, by Confederates

Antietam
Bull Run
Seven Days' Battles
Wilderness
Norfolk
Raleigh
New Bern

17 September 1862 Union victory

21 July 1861 Confederate victory

9 April 1865 Main Confederate surrender

Appomattox

13 April 1865 Occupied by Union

Columbia
Fort Sumter
Port Royal Sound
Savannah
Fort Pulaski

Fernandina
Jacksonville
St Augustine

22 December 1864 Occupied by Union

Atlanta

2 September 1864 Occupied by Union

16 February 1862 Union victory

25 November 1863 Union victory

Chattanooga
Tennessee

Fort Donelson
Shiloh

7 April 1862 Union victory

Ship Island
Fort St Philip

New Orleans

26 April 1862 Occupied by Union

4 July 1863 6 weeks siege Union victory

Vicksburg

Mississippi

Potomac

0   200
Miles

56

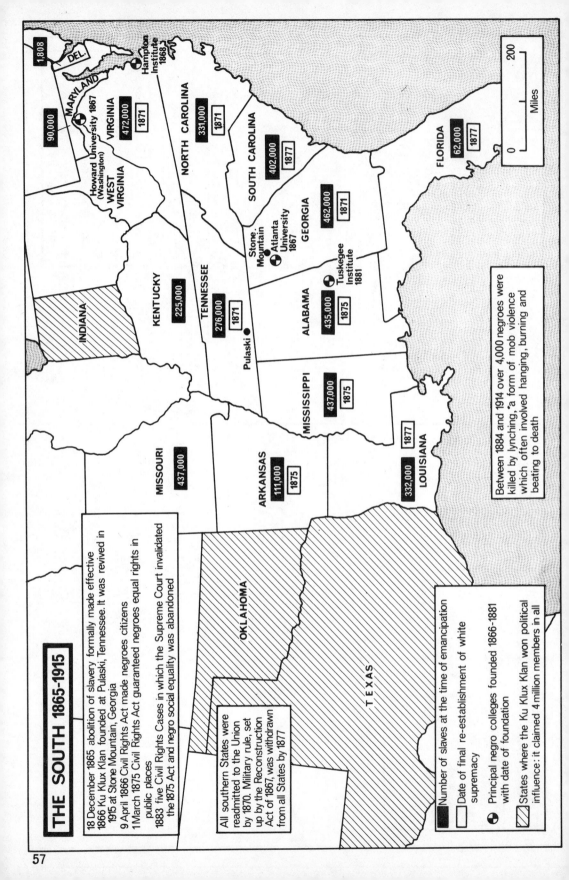

THE SOUTH 1865-1915

18 December 1865 abolition of slavery formally made effective
1866 Ku Klux Klan founded at Pulaski, Tennessee. It was revived in 1915 at Stone Mountain, Georgia
9 April 1866 Civil Rights Act made negroes citizens
1 March 1875 Civil Rights Act guaranteed negroes equal rights in public places
1883 five Civil Rights Cases in which the Supreme Court invalidated the 1875 Act and negro social equality was abandoned

All southern States were readmitted to the Union by 1870. Military rule, set up by the Reconstruction Act of 1867, was withdrawn from all States by 1877

Between 1884 and 1914 over 4,000 negroes were killed by lynching, a form of mob violence which often involved hanging, burning and beating to death

Number of slaves at the time of emancipation

Date of final re-establishment of white supremacy

Principal negro colleges founded 1866-1881 with date of foundation

States where the Ku Klux Klan won political influence: it claimed 4 million members in all

1,808 DEL.
Hampton Institute 1868
90,000 MARYLAND
Howard University (Washington) 1867
WEST VIRGINIA
472,000 VIRGINIA 1871
331,000 NORTH CAROLINA 1871
402,000 SOUTH CAROLINA 1877
62,000 FLORIDA 1877
GEORGIA 462,000 1871
Stone Mountain
Atlanta University 1867
Tuskegee Institute 1881
435,000 ALABAMA 1875
225,000 KENTUCKY
276,000 TENNESSEE 1871
Pulaski
INDIANA
437,000 MISSISSIPPI 1875
437,000 MISSOURI
111,000 ARKANSAS 1875
332,000 LOUISIANA 1877
OKLAHOMA
TEXAS

Miles
0 200

57

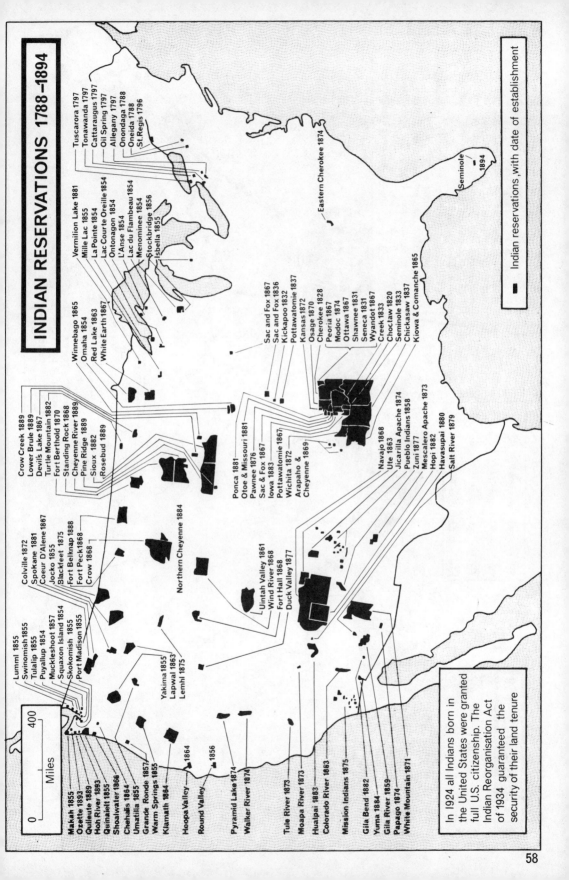

INDIAN RESERVATIONS 1788–1894

Tuscarora 1797
Tonawanda 1797
Cattaraugus 1797
Oil Spring 1797
Allegany 1797
Onondaga 1788
Oneida 1788
St. Regis 1796

Eastern Cherokee 1874

Seminole
1894

Vermilion Lake 1881
Mille Lac 1855
La Pointe 1854
Lac Courte Oreille 1854
Ontonagon 1854
L'Anse 1854
Lac du Flambeau 1854
Menominee 1854
Stockbridge 1856
Isbella 1855

Winnebago 1865
Omaha 1854
Red Lake 1863
White Earth 1867

Sac and Fox 1867
Sac and Fox 1836
Kickapoo 1832
Pottawatomie 1837
Kansas 1872
Cherokee 1828
Osage 1870
Modoc 1874
Peoria 1867
Ottawa 1867
Shawnee 1831
Seneca 1831
Wyandot 1867
Choctaw 1820
Creek 1833
Seminole 1833
Chickasaw 1837
Kiowa & Comanche 1865

Crow Creek 1889
Lower Brule 1889
Devils Lake 1867
Turtle Mountain 1882
Fort Berthold 1870
Standing Rock 1889
Cheyenne River 1889
Pine Ridge 1889
Sioux 1882
Rosebud 1889

Ponca 1881
Otoe & Missouri 1881
Pawnee 1876
Sac & Fox 1867
Iowa 1883
Wichita 1872
Pottawatomie 1867
Arapaho &
Cheyenne 1869

Navajo 1868
Ute 1863
Jicarilla Apache 1874
Pueblo Indians 1858
Zuni 1877
Mescalero Apache 1873
Hopi 1882
Havasupai 1880
Salt River 1879

Colville 1872
Spokane 1881
Coeur D'Alene 1887
Jocko 1855
Blackfeet 1875
Fort Belknap 1888
Crow 1868

Northern Cheyenne 1884

Lumml 1855
Swinomish 1855
Tulalip 1855
Puyallup 1854
Muckleshoot 1857
Squaxon Island 1854
Skokomish 1855
Port Madison 1855

Yakima 1855
Lapwal 1863
Lemhi 1875

Uintah Valley 1861
Wind River 1868
Fort Hall 1868
Duck Valley 1877

Hoopa Valley

Round Valley

1864

1856

Pyramid Lake 1874
Walker River 1874

Makah 1855
Ozette 1893
Quileute 1889
Hoh River 1893
Quinaielt 1855
Shoalwater 1866
Chehalis 1864
Umatilla 1855
Grande Ronde 1857
Warm Springs 1855
Klamath 1864

Tule River 1873
Moapa River 1873

Huaipai 1883
Colorado River 1863

Mission Indians 1875

Gila Bend 1882
Yuma 1884
Gila River 1859
Papago 1874
White Mountain 1871

0   400
Miles

In 1924 all Indians born in
the United States were granted
full U.S. citizenship. The
Indian Reorganisation Act
of 1934 guaranteed the
security of their land tenure

■ Indian reservations, with date of establishment

58

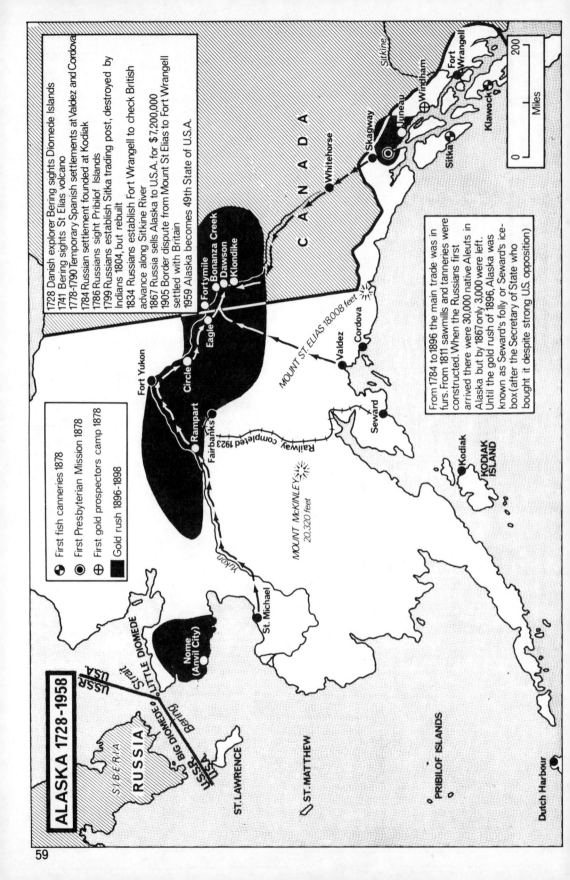

ALASKA 1728-1958

RUSSIA
SIBERIA
USSR
USA
BIG DIOMEDE
LITTLE DIOMEDE
Bering Strait
CANADA

1728 Danish explorer Bering sights Diomede Islands
1741 Bering sights St Elias volcano
1778-1790 Temporary Spanish settlements at Valdez and Cordova
1784 Russian settlement founded at Kodiak
1786 Russians sight Pribilof Islands
1799 Russians establish Sitka trading post, destroyed by Indians 1804, but rebuilt
1834 Russians establish Fort Wrangell to check British advance along Sitkine River
1867 Russia sells Alaska to U.S.A. for $7,200,000
1905 Border dispute from Mount St Elias to Fort Wrangell settled with Britain
1959 Alaska becomes 49th State of U.S.A.

From 1784 to 1896 the main trade was in furs. From 1811 sawmills and tanneries were constructed. When the Russians first arrived there were 30,000 native Aleuts in Alaska but by 1867 only 3,000 were left. Until the gold rush of 1896, Alaska was known as Seward's folly or Seward's icebox (after the Secretary of State who bought it despite strong U.S. opposition)

⊕ First fish canneries 1878
◉ First Presbyterian Mission 1878
⊕ First gold prospectors camp 1878
■ Gold rush 1896-1898

200
0
Miles

Sitkine
Fort Wrangell
Windham
Juneau
Skagway
Klawock
Whitehorse
Sitka

Fort Yukon
Eagle
Fortymile
Bonanza Creek
Dawson
Klondike
Circle
Rampart
Fairbanks
Railway completed 1923
MOUNT ST ELIAS 18,008 feet
Valdez
Cordova
Seward

MOUNT McKINLEY
20,320 feet

Yukon
St. Michael

Nome (Anvil City)

Kodiak
KODIAK ISLAND

ST. LAWRENCE
ST. MATTHEW
PRIBILOF ISLANDS
Dutch Harbour

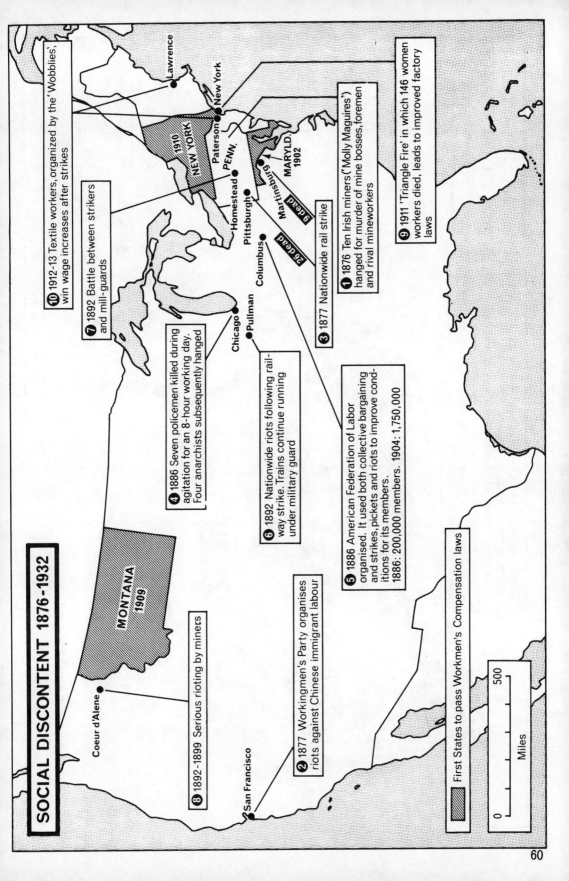

SOCIAL DISCONTENT 1876-1932

❶ 1876 Ten Irish miners ('Molly Maguires') hanged for murder of mine bosses, foremen and rival mineworkers

❷ 1877 Workingmen's Party organises riots against Chinese immigrant labour

❸ 1877 Nationwide rail strike

❹ 1886 Seven policemen killed during agitation for an 8-hour working day. Four anarchists subsequently hanged

❺ 1886 American Federation of Labor organised. It used both collective bargaining and strikes, pickets and riots to improve conditions for its members. 1886: 200,000 members. 1904: 1,750,000

❻ 1892 Nationwide riots following railway strike. Trains continue running under military guard

❼ 1892 Battle between strikers and mill-guards

❽ 1892-1899 Serious rioting by miners

❾ 1911 'Triangle Fire' in which 146 women workers died, leads to improved factory laws

❿ 1912-13 Textile workers, organized by the 'Wobblies', win wage increases after strikes

MONTANA 1909

NEW YORK 1910

PENN. MARYLD. 1902

9 dead

26 dead

Coeur d'Alene

San Francisco

Chicago

Pullman

Columbus

Pittsburgh

Homestead

Martinsburg

Paterson

New York

Lawrence

First States to pass Workmen's Compensation laws

Miles

0   500

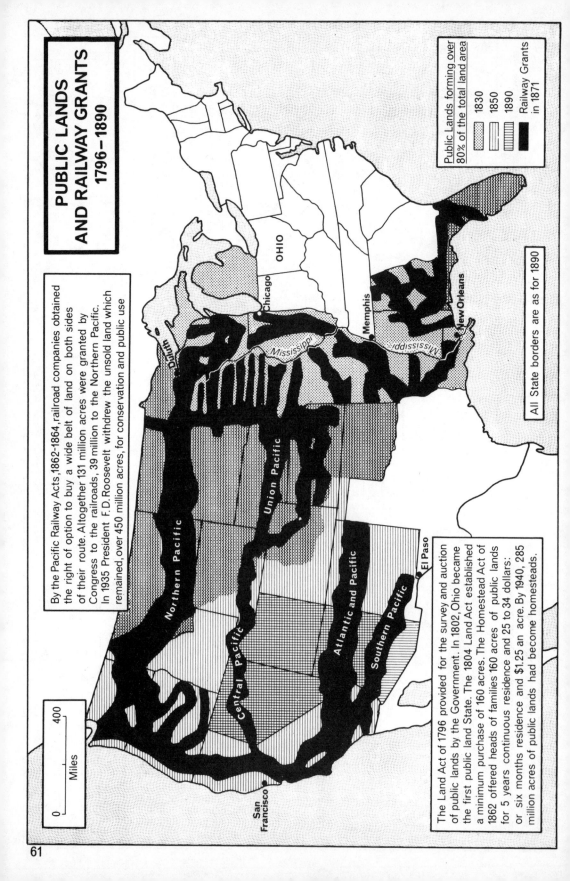

PUBLIC LANDS AND RAILWAY GRANTS 1796–1890

By the Pacific Railway Acts,1862-1864,railroad companies obtained the right of option to buy a wide belt of land on both sides of their route. Altogether 131 million acres were granted by Congress to the railroads, 39 million to the Northern Pacific. In 1935 President F.D.Roosevelt withdrew the unsold land which remained, over 450 million acres, for conservation and public use

The Land Act of 1796 provided for the survey and auction of public lands by the Government. In 1802, Ohio became the first public land State. The 1804 Land Act established a minimum purchase of 160 acres. The Homestead Act of 1862 offered heads of families 160 acres of public lands for 5 years continuous residence and 25 to 34 dollars; or six months residence and $1.25 an acre. By 1940, 285 million acres of public lands had become homesteads.

All State borders are as for 1890

Public Lands forming over 80% of the total land area

1830

1850

1890

Railway Grants in 1871

Northern Pacific

Union Pacific

Central Pacific

Atlantic and Pacific

Southern Pacific

OHIO

Mississippi

Mississippi

Duluth

Chicago

Memphis

New Orleans

El Paso

San Francisco

0   400

Miles

61

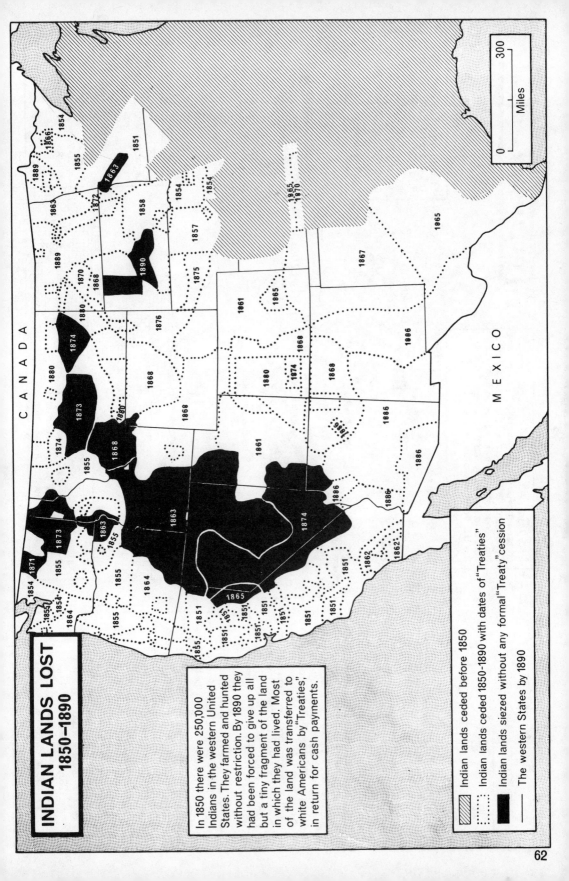

INDIAN LANDS LOST 1850–1890

In 1850 there were 250,000 Indians in the western United States. They farmed and hunted without restriction. By 1890 they had been forced to give up all but a tiny fragment of the land in which they had lived. Most of the land was transferred to white Americans by "Treaties", in return for cash payments.

CANADA

MEXICO

0   300
Miles

Indian lands ceded before 1850

Indian lands ceded 1850-1890 with dates of "Treaties"

Indian lands siezed without any formal "Treaty" cession

The western States by 1890

62

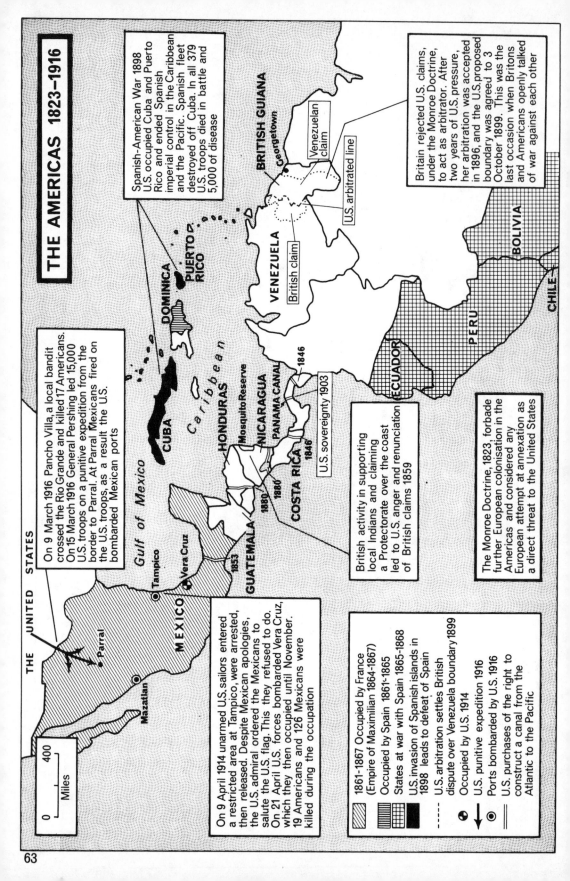

THE AMERICAS 1823–1916

Spanish-American War 1898 U.S. occupied Cuba and Puerto Rico and ended Spanish imperial control in the Caribbean and the Pacific. Spanish fleet destroyed off Cuba. In all 379 U.S. troops died in battle and 5,000 of disease

Britain rejected U.S. claims, under the Monroe Doctrine, to act as arbitrator. After two years of U.S. pressure, her arbitration was accepted in 1896, and the U.S. proposed boundary was agreed to 3 October 1899. This was the last occasion when Britons and Americans openly talked of war against each other

BRITISH GUIANA
Georgetown

Venezuelan claim

U.S. arbitrated line

VENEZUELA

British claim

BOLIVIA

ECUADOR

PERU

CHILE

On 9 March 1916 Pancho Villa, a local bandit crossed the Rio Grande and killed 17 Americans. On 15 March 1916 General Pershing led 15,000 U.S. troops on a punitive expedition from the border to Parral. At Parral Mexicans fired on the U.S. troops, as a result the U.S. bombarded Mexican ports

DOMINICA

PUERTO RICO

Caribbean

CUBA

1846

HONDURAS
Mosquito Reserve

NICARAGUA
PANAMA CANAL

COSTA RICA
1846

U.S. sovereignty 1903

British activity in supporting local Indians and claiming a Protectorate over the coast led to U.S. anger and renunciation of British claims 1859

THE UNITED STATES

Gulf of Mexico

Tampico
Vera Cruz

1853

GUATEMALA

1880
1880

Parral

MEXICO

Mazatlan

On 9 April 1914 unarmed U.S. sailors entered a restricted area at Tampico, were arrested, then released. Despite Mexican apologies, the U.S. admiral ordered the Mexicans to salute the U.S. flag. This they refused to do. On 21 April U.S. forces bombarded Vera Cruz, which they then occupied until November. 19 Americans and 126 Mexicans were killed during the occupation

The Monroe Doctrine, 1823, forbade further European colonisation in the Americas and considered any European attempt at annexation as a direct threat to the United States

0   400
Miles

1861–1867 Occupied by France (Empire of Maximilian 1864–1867)

Occupied by Spain 1861–1865

States at war with Spain 1865–1868

U.S. invasion of Spanish islands in 1898 leads to defeat of Spain

U.S. arbitration settles British dispute over Venezuela boundary 1899

Occupied by U.S. 1914

U.S. punitive expedition 1916

Ports bombarded by U.S. 1916

U.S. purchases of the right to construct a canal from the Atlantic to the Pacific

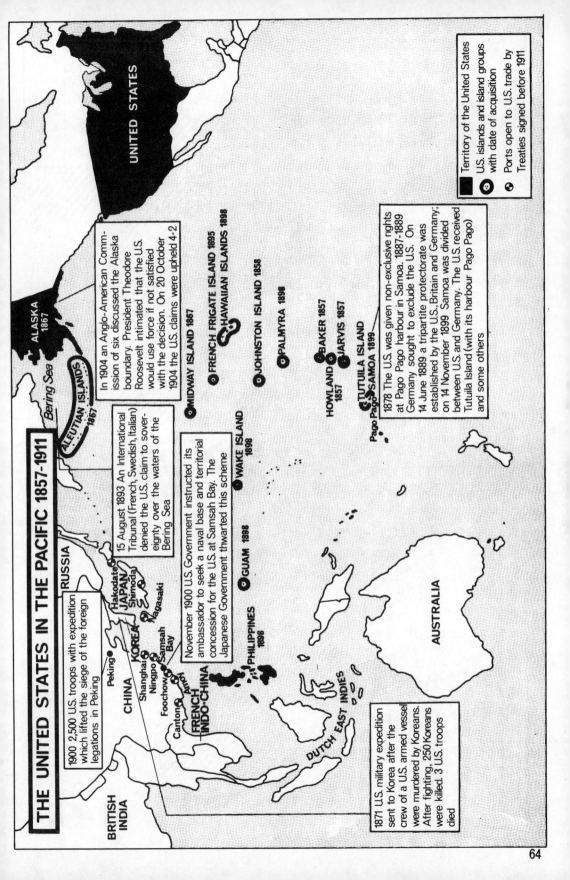

THE UNITED STATES IN THE PACIFIC 1857-1911

RUSSIA

UNITED STATES

ALASKA 1867

Bering Sea

ALEUTIAN ISLANDS 1867

1900 2,500 U.S. troops with expedition which lifted the siege of the foreign legations in Peking

15 August 1893 An International Tribunal (French, Swedish, Italian) denied the U.S. claim to sovereignty over the waters of the Bering Sea

In 1904 an Anglo-American Commission of six discussed the Alaska boundary. President Theodore Roosevelt intimated that the U.S. would use force if not satisfied with the decision. On 20 October 1904 the U.S. claims were upheld 4-2

November 1900 U.S. Government instructed its ambassador to seek a naval base and territorial concession for the U.S. at Samsah Bay. The Japanese Government thwarted this scheme

BRITISH INDIA

CHINA

Peking

Shanghai
Ningpo
Foochow
Amoy
Canton

FRENCH INDO-CHINA

KOREA

Samsah Bay

JAPAN

Hakodate
Shimoda
Nagasaki

PHILIPPINES 1898

GUAM 1898

WAKE ISLAND 1898

MIDWAY ISLAND 1867

FRENCH FRIGATE ISLAND 1895

HAWAIIAN ISLANDS 1898

JOHNSTON ISLAND 1858

PALMYRA 1898

HOWLAND 1857

BAKER 1857

JARVIS 1857

TUTUILA ISLAND
Pago Pago **SAMOA 1899**

1878 The U.S. was given non-exclusive rights at Pago Pago harbour in Samoa. 1887-1889 Germany sought to exclude the U.S. On 14 June 1889 a tripartite protectorate was established by the U.S., Britain and Germany; on 14 November 1899 Samoa was divided between U.S. and Germany. The U.S. received Tutuila Island (with its harbour Pago Pago) and some others

1871 U.S. military expedition sent to Korea after the crew of a U.S. armed vessel were murdered by Koreans. After fighting, 250 Koreans were killed. 3 U.S. troops died

DUTCH EAST INDIES

AUSTRALIA

Territory of the United States

U.S. islands and island groups with date of acquisition

Ports open to U.S. trade by Treaties signed before 1911

64

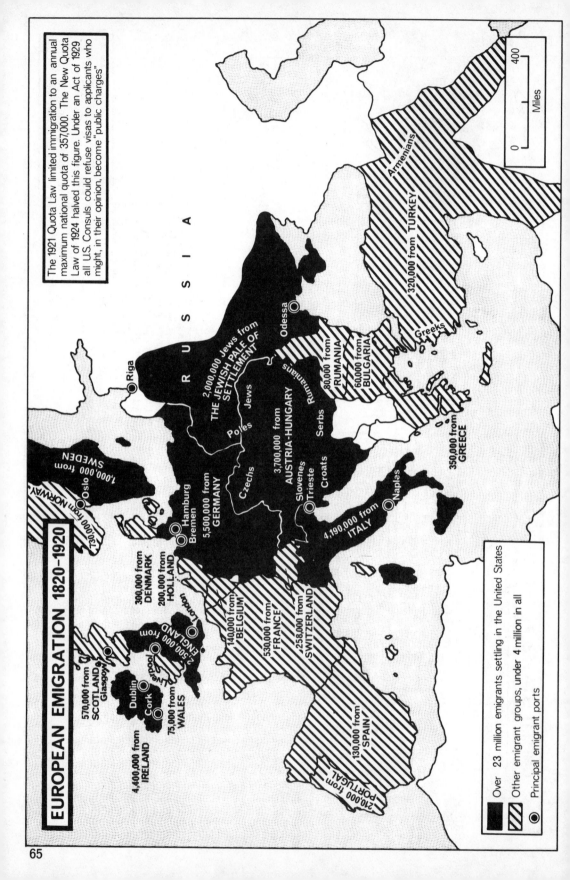

EUROPEAN EMIGRATION 1820–1920

The 1921 Quota Law limited immigration to an annual maximum national quota of 357,000. The New Quota Law of 1924 halved this figure. Under an Act of 1929 all U.S. Consuls could refuse visas to applicants who might, in their opinion, become "public charges"

R U S S I A

2,000,000 Jews from THE JEWISH PALE OF SETTLEMENT

Riga

Odessa

320,000 from TURKEY

Armenians

Greeks

80,000 from RUMANIA

60,000 from BULGARIA

Rumanians

350,000 from GREECE

Poles

Jews

Czechs

3,700,000 from AUSTRIA-HUNGARY

Serbs

Slovenes

Croats

Trieste

4,190,000 from ITALY

Naples

1,000,000 from SWEDEN

Oslo

73,000 from NORWAY

Hamburg

Bremen

5,500,000 from GERMANY

300,000 from DENMARK

200,000 from HOLLAND

140,000 from BELGIUM

530,000 from FRANCE

258,000 from SWITZERLAND

130,000 from SPAIN

210,000 from PORTUGAL

570,000 from SCOTLAND

Glasgow

2,500,000 from ENGLAND

London

Liverpool

75,000 from WALES

4,400,000 from IRELAND

Dublin

Cork

0   400
Miles

■ Over 23 million emigrants settling in the United States

▨ Other emigrant groups, under 4 million in all

◎ Principal emigrant ports

65

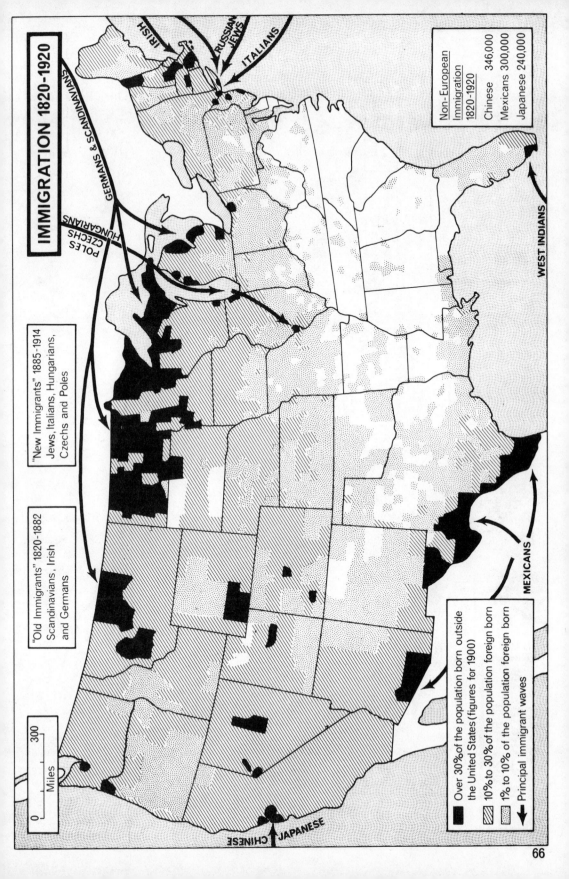

IMMIGRATION 1820-1920

Non-European
Immigration
1820-1920

Chinese   346,000
Mexicans 300,000
Japanese   240,000

"New Immigrants" 1885-1914
Jews, Italians, Hungarians,
Czechs and Poles

"Old Immigrants" 1820-1882
Scandinavians, Irish
and Germans

IRISH

RUSSIAN JEWS

ITALIANS

GERMANS & SCANDINAVIANS

POLES
CZECHS
HUNGARIANS

WEST INDIANS

MEXICANS

CHINESE JAPANESE

■ Over 30% of the population born outside
   the United States (figures for 1900)

▨ 10% to 30% of the population foreign born

░ 1% to 10% of the population foreign born

→ Principal immigrant waves

300
Miles
0

66

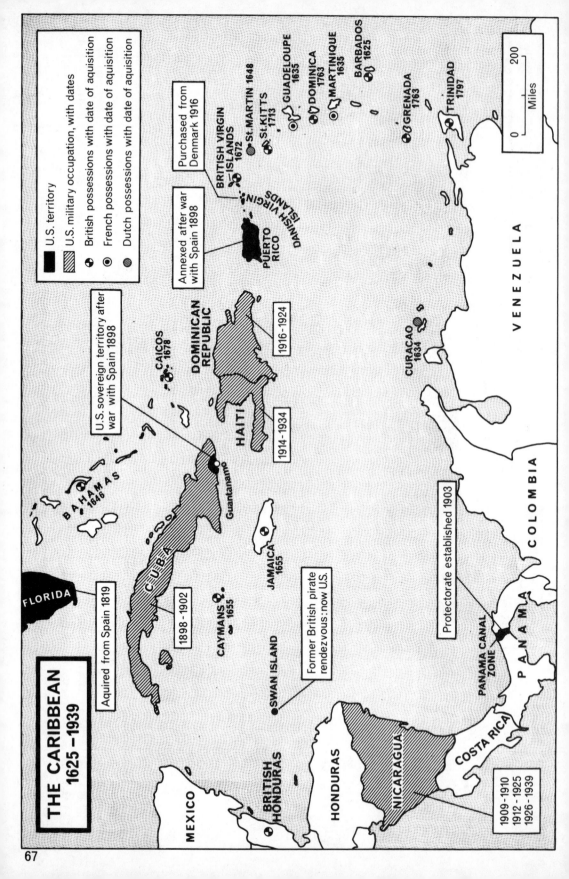

THE CARIBBEAN
1625 –1939

U.S. territory

U.S. military occupation, with dates

British possessions with date of aquisition

French possessions with date of aquisition

Dutch possessions with date of aquisition

Purchased from Denmark 1916

Annexed after war with Spain 1898

BRITISH VIRGIN ISLANDS 1672

DANISH VIRGIN ISLANDS

St. MARTIN 1648

St. KITTS 1713

GUADELOUPE 1635

DOMINICA 1763

MARTINIQUE 1635

BARBADOS 1625

GRENADA 1763

TRINIDAD 1797

200

0   Miles

PUERTO RICO

U.S. sovereign territory after war with Spain 1898

DOMINICAN REPUBLIC

1916 - 1924

CAICOS 1678

HAITI

1914 - 1934

CURACAO 1634

FLORIDA

Aquired from Spain 1819

BAHAMAS 1646

CUBA

Guantanamo

1898 - 1902

CAYMANS 1655

JAMAICA 1655

Former British pirate rendezvous: now U.S.

SWAN ISLAND

VENEZUELA

COLOMBIA

Protectorate established 1903

PANAMA CANAL ZONE

PANAMA

COSTA RICA

NICARAGUA

1909 - 1910
1912 - 1925
1926 - 1939

MEXICO

BRITISH HONDURAS

HONDURAS

THE PANAMA CANAL ZONE PROTECTORATE 1903

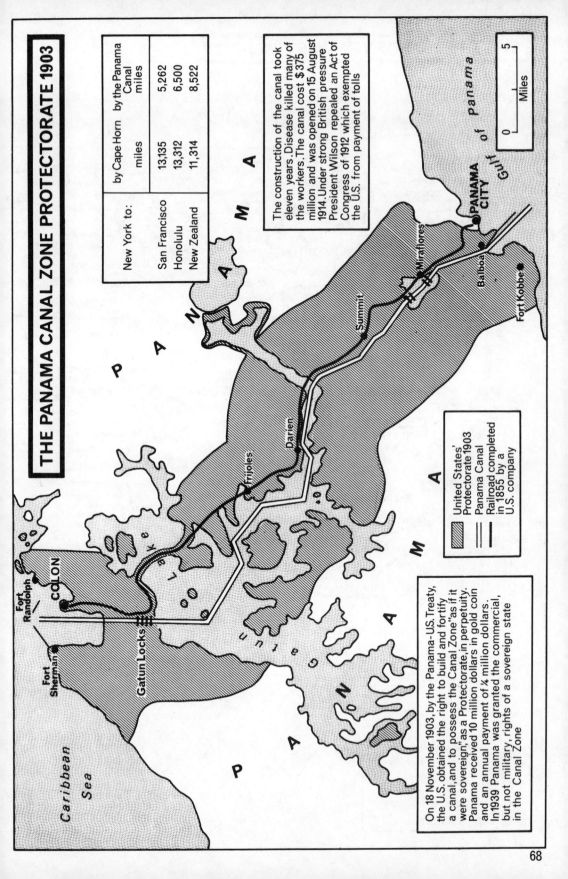

New York to:	by Cape Horn miles	by the Panama Canal miles
San Francisco	13,135	5,262
Honolulu	13,312	6,500
New Zealand	11,314	8,522

The construction of the canal took eleven years. Disease killed many of the workers. The canal cost $375 million and was opened on 15 August 1914. Under strong British pressure President Wilson repealed an Act of Congress of 1912 which exempted the U.S. from payment of tolls

Caribbean Sea

Fort Randolph
Fort Sherman
COLON
Gatun Locks

Frijoles

Darien

Summit

Miraflores

PANAMA CITY

Balboa

Fort Kobbe

Gulf of Panama

PANAMA

P A N A M A

Legend

United States' Protectorate 1903

Panama Canal

Railroad completed in 1855 by a U.S. company

0   5
Miles

On 18 November 1903, by the Panama-U.S. Treaty, the U.S. obtained the right to build and fortify a canal, and to possess the Canal Zone "as if it were sovereign," as a Protectorate, in perpetuity. Panama received 10 million dollars in gold coin and an annual payment of ¼ million dollars. In 1939 Panama was granted the commercial, but not military, rights of a sovereign state in the Canal Zone

68

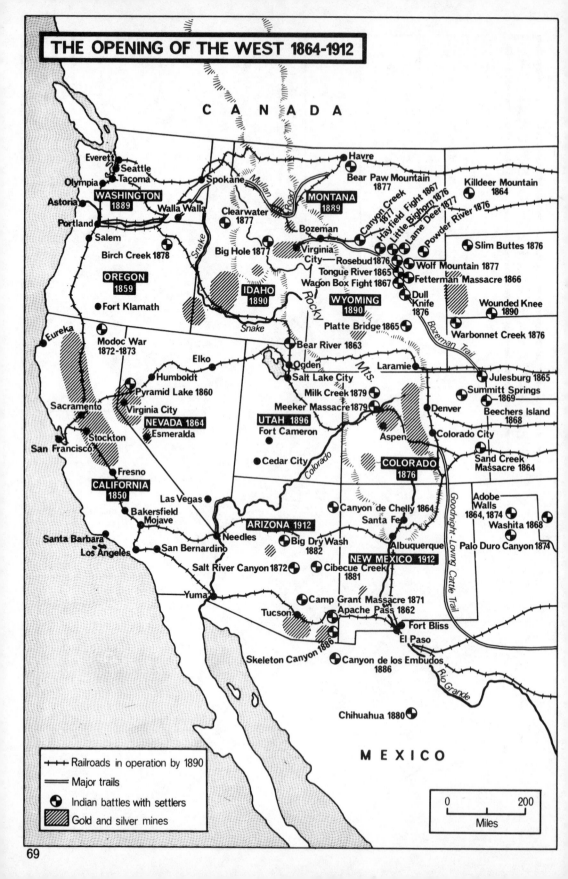

THE OPENING OF THE WEST 1864-1912

CANADA

Everett
Seattle
Tacoma
Olympia
Spokane
Astoria
WASHINGTON 1889
Walla Walla
Portland
Salem
Birch Creek 1878
OREGON 1859
Fort Klamath

Havre
Bear Paw Mountain 1877
Killdeer Mountain 1864
Clearwater 1877
Mullan Road
MONTANA 1889
Bozeman
Canyon Creek 1877
Hayfield Fight 1867
Little Bighorn 1876
Lame Deer 1877
Powder River 1876
Slim Buttes 1876
Big Hole 1877
Virginia City
Rosebud 1876
Wolf Mountain 1877
Tongue River 1865
Fetterman Massacre 1866
Wagon Box Fight 1867
IDAHO 1890
Snake
Dull Knife 1876
Wounded Knee 1890
WYOMING 1890
Platte Bridge 1865
Warbonnet Creek 1876
Bozeman Trail

Eureka
Modoc War 1872-1873
Bear River 1863
Elko
Humboldt
Ogden
Laramie
Julesburg 1865
Pyramid Lake 1860
Salt Lake City
Milk Creek 1879
Summitt Springs 1869
Sacramento
Virginia City
Meeker Massacre 1879
Denver
Beechers Island 1868
NEVADA 1864
Esmeralda
UTAH 1896
Fort Cameron
Aspen
Colorado City
Stockton
San Francisco
Cedar City
COLORADO 1876
Sand Creek Massacre 1864
Fresno
CALIFORNIA 1850
Las Vegas
Colorado
Adobe Walls 1864, 1874
Bakersfield
Mojave
ARIZONA 1912
Canyon de Chelly 1864
Santa Fe
Washita 1868
Santa Barbara
San Bernardino
Needles
Big Dry Wash 1882
Albuquerque
Palo Duro Canyon 1874
Los Angeles
Salt River Canyon 1872
Cibecue Creek 1881
NEW MEXICO 1912
Goodnight-Loving Cattle Trail
Yuma
Camp Grant Massacre 1871
Tucson
Apache Pass 1862
Fort Bliss
El Paso
Skeleton Canyon 1886
Canyon de los Embudos 1886
Rio Grande

Chihuahua 1880

MEXICO

Snake
Rocky
Mtts.

+++	Railroads in operation by 1890
===	Major trails
◑	Indian battles with settlers
░░	Gold and silver mines

0   200
Miles

69

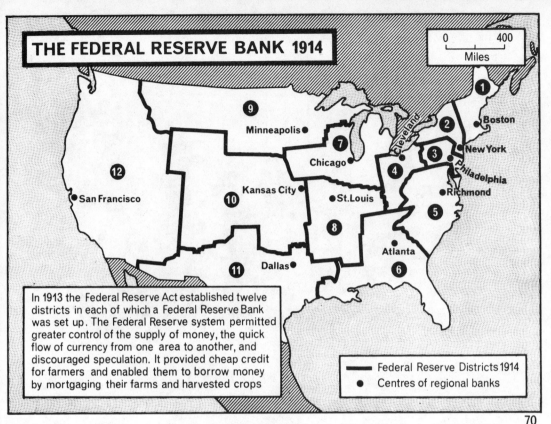

THE FEDERAL RESERVE BANK 1914

0   400
Miles

①

② Boston

New York

③ Philadelphia

Cleveland

⑨ Minneapolis

⑦ Chicago

④ ⑤ Richmond

⑫ San Francisco

Kansas City ⑩

St.Louis

⑧

Atlanta

⑥

⑪ Dallas

In 1913 the Federal Reserve Act established twelve districts in each of which a Federal Reserve Bank was set up. The Federal Reserve system permitted greater control of the supply of money, the quick flow of currency from one area to another, and discouraged speculation. It provided cheap credit for farmers and enabled them to borrow money by mortgaging their farms and harvested crops

— Federal Reserve Districts 1914
• Centres of regional banks

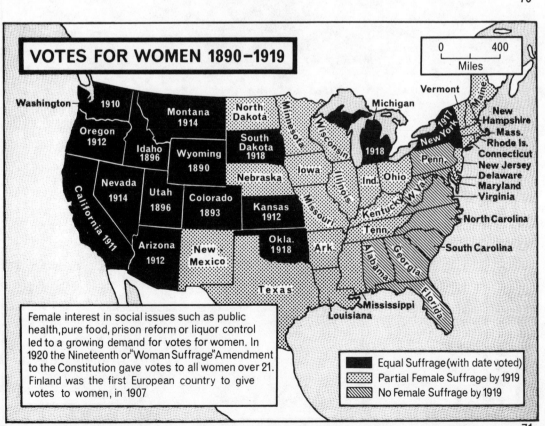

VOTES FOR WOMEN 1890–1919

0   400
Miles

Washington 1910

Oregon 1912

Montana 1914

North Dakota

Minnesota

Wisconsin

Michigan

Vermont

Maine

1917 New York

New Hampshire

Mass.

Rhode Is.

Connecticut

New Jersey

Delaware

Maryland

Virginia

Idaho 1896

Wyoming 1890

South Dakota 1918

Iowa

Nebraska

Illinois

Ind.

Ohio

Penn

1918

W.Va

Nevada 1914

Utah 1896

Colorado 1893

Kansas 1912

Missouri

Kentucky

Tenn.

North Carolina

California 1911

Arizona 1912

New Mexico

Okla. 1918

Ark

Alabama

Georgia

South Carolina

Texas

Mississippi

Louisiana

Florida

Female interest in social issues such as public health, pure food, prison reform or liquor control led to a growing demand for votes for women. In 1920 the Nineteenth or "Woman Suffrage" Amendment to the Constitution gave votes to all women over 21. Finland was the first European country to give votes to women, in 1907

■ Equal Suffrage (with date voted)
▦ Partial Female Suffrage by 1919
▨ No Female Suffrage by 1919

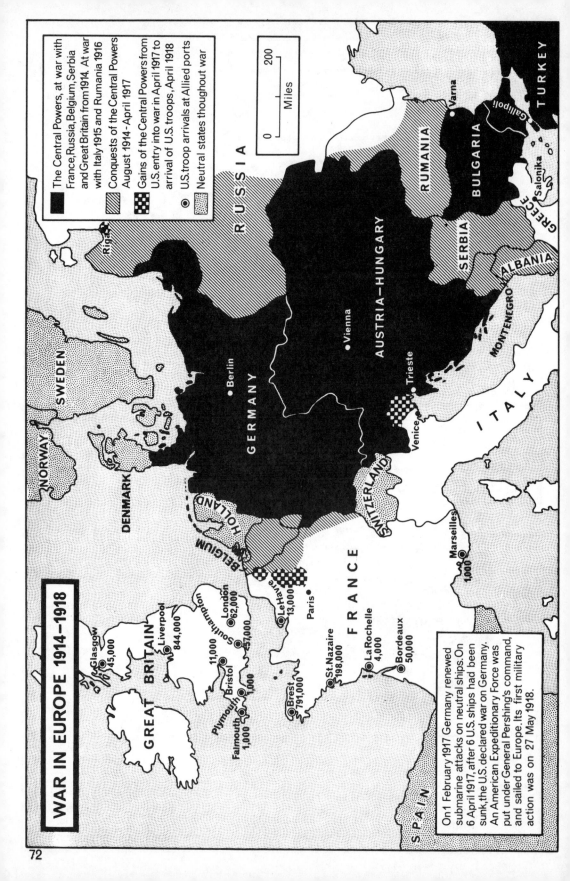

WAR IN EUROPE 1914–1918

Legend:

■ The Central Powers, at war with France, Russia, Belgium, Serbia and Great Britain from 1914. At war with Italy 1915 and Rumania 1916

▨ Conquests of the Central Powers August 1914–April 1917

▧ Gains of the Central Powers from U.S. entry into war in April 1917 to arrival of U.S. troops, April 1918

◉ U.S. troop arrivals at Allied ports

░ Neutral states thoughout war

0 — 200 Miles

Labels: NORWAY, SWEDEN, DENMARK, GREAT BRITAIN, HOLLAND, BELGIUM, FRANCE, SPAIN, SWITZERLAND, GERMANY, RUSSIA, AUSTRIA–HUNGARY, ITALY, MONTENEGRO, ALBANIA, SERBIA, BULGARIA, RUMANIA, GREECE, TURKEY

Berlin • , Vienna • , Trieste • , Venice • , Riga • , Varna • , Gallipoli • , Salonika • , Paris • , Marseilles • , Le Havre • , Bordeaux •

Glasgow 45,000
Liverpool 844,000
Bristol 11,000
London 62,000
Southampton 57,000
Plymouth 1,000
Falmouth 1,000
Brest 791,000
St.Nazaire 198,000
La Rochelle 4,000
Bordeaux 50,000
Le Havre 13,000
Marseilles 1,000

On 1 February 1917 Germany renewed submarine attacks on neutral ships. On 6 April 1917, after 6 U.S. ships had been sunk, the U.S. declared war on Germany. An American Expeditionary Force was put under General Pershing's command, and sailed to Europe. Its first military action was on 27 May 1918.

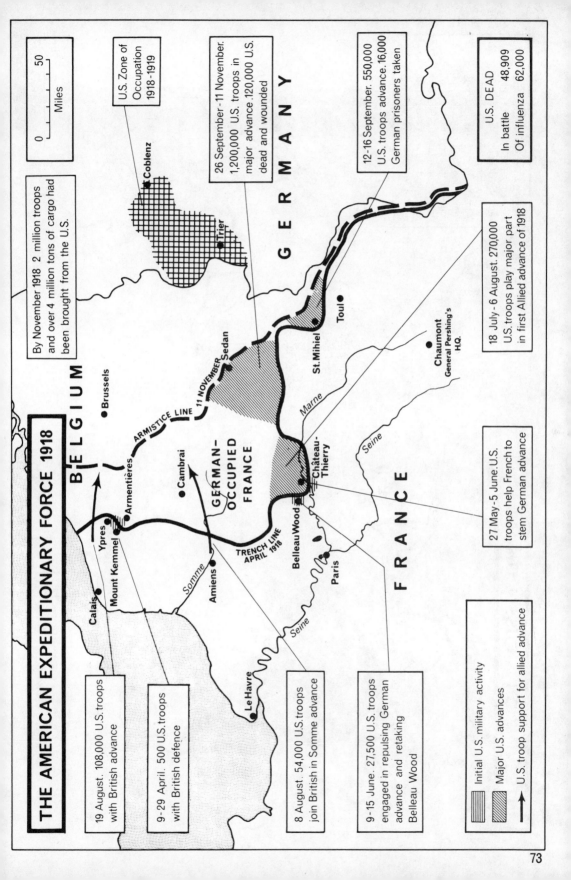

THE AMERICAN EXPEDITIONARY FORCE 1918

U.S. Zone of Occupation 1918-1919

By November 1918 2 million troops and over 4 million tons of cargo had been brought from the U.S.

26 September-11 November. 1,200,000 U.S. troops in major advance. 120,000 U.S. dead and wounded

12-16 September. 550,000 U.S. troops advance. 16,000 German prisoners taken

U.S. DEAD
In battle   48,909
Of influenza   62,000

18 July - 6 August. 270,000 U.S. troops play major part in first Allied advance of 1918

27 May-5 June. U.S. troops help French to stem German advance

19 August. 108,000 U.S. troops with British advance

9-29 April. 500 U.S. troops with British defence

8 August. 54,000 U.S. troops join British in Somme advance

9-15 June. 27,500 U.S. troops engaged in repulsing German advance and retaking Belleau Wood

GERMANY

BELGIUM

FRANCE

GERMAN-OCCUPIED FRANCE

ARMISTICE LINE

11 NOVEMBER

TRENCH LINE APRIL 1918

50

Miles

0

Coblenz

Trier

Toul

Chaumont
General Pershing's H.Q.

Brussels

Sedan

St. Mihiel

Château-Thierry

Cambrai

Armentières

Ypres

Mount Kemmel

Calais

Amiens

Le Havre

Paris

Belleau Wood

Marne

Seine

Seine

Somme

Initial U.S. military activity

Major U.S. advances

U.S. troop support for allied advance

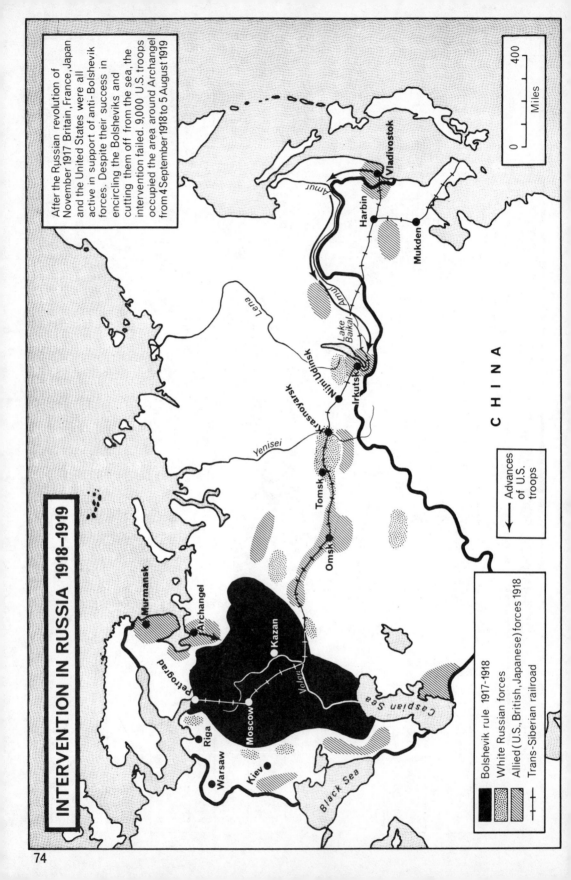

INTERVENTION IN RUSSIA 1918–1919

After the Russian revolution of November 1917 Britain, France, Japan and the United States were all active in support of anti-Bolshevik forces. Despite their success in encircling the Bolsheviks and cutting them off from the sea, the intervention failed. 9,000 U.S. troops occupied the area around Archangel from 4 September 1918 to 5 August 1919.

Murmansk
Archangel
Petrograd
Riga
Warsaw
Kiev
Moscow
Kazan
Volga
Black Sea
Caspian Sea
Omsk
Tomsk
Krasnoyarsk
Yenisei
Nijni Udinsk
Irkutsk
Lake Baikal
Lena
Amur
Harbin
Mukden
Vladivostok
CHINA

Advances of U.S. troops

Bolshevik rule 1917–1918
White Russian forces
Allied (U.S., British, Japanese) forces 1918
Trans-Siberian railroad

0   400
Miles

74

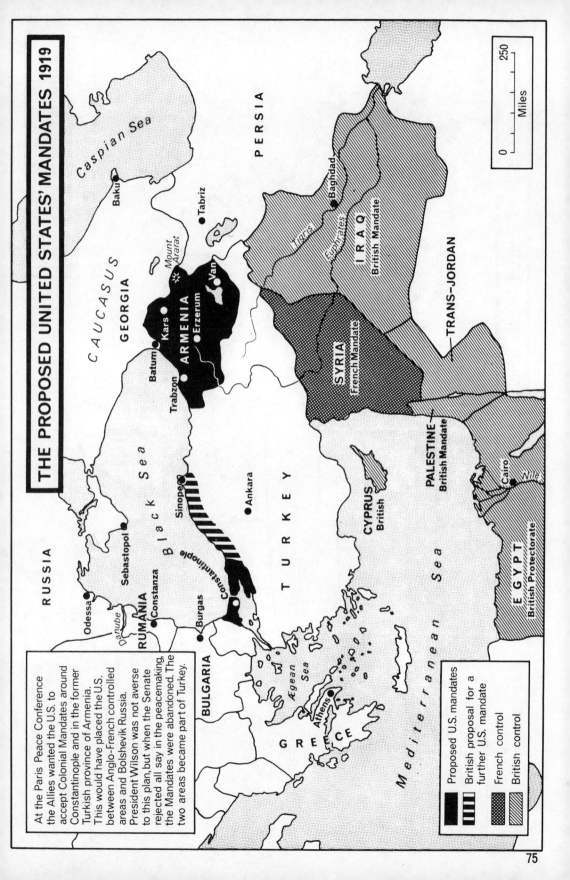

THE PROPOSED UNITED STATES' MANDATES 1919

At the Paris Peace Conference the Allies wanted the U.S. to accept Colonial Mandates around Constantinople and in the former Turkish province of Armenia. This would have placed the U.S. between Anglo-French controlled areas and Bolshevik Russia. President Wilson was not averse to this plan, but when the Senate rejected all say in the peacemaking, the Mandates were abandoned. The two areas became part of Turkey.

Proposed U.S. mandates

British proposal for a further U.S. mandate

French control

British control

PERSIA

Caspian Sea

Baku

Tabriz

Mount Ararat

Van

ARMENIA

Kars   Erzerum

GEORGIA

Batum

CAUCASUS

Trabzon

RUSSIA

Black Sea

Odessa

Sebastopol

RUMANIA

Constanza

Burgas

Danube

BULGARIA

Sinope

Constantinople

Ankara

T U R K E Y

Baghdad

Euphrates

Tigris

I R A Q
British Mandate

TRANS-JORDAN

SYRIA
French Mandate

PALESTINE
British Mandate

CYPRUS
British

Cairo

Nile

E G Y P T
British Protectorate

Aegean Sea

Athens

G R E E C E

Mediterranean Sea

250

0

Miles

75

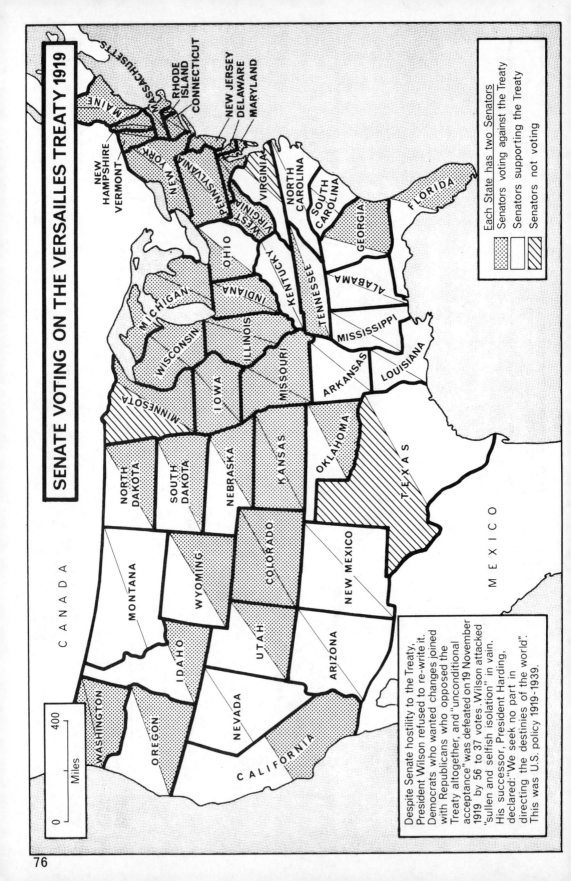

SENATE VOTING ON THE VERSAILLES TREATY 1919

CANADA

WASHINGTON
OREGON
MONTANA
IDAHO
WYOMING
NORTH DAKOTA
SOUTH DAKOTA
MINNESOTA
NEVADA
UTAH
COLORADO
NEBRASKA
IOWA
WISCONSIN
MICHIGAN
CALIFORNIA
ARIZONA
NEW MEXICO
KANSAS
OKLAHOMA
MISSOURI
ILLINOIS
INDIANA
OHIO
TEXAS
ARKANSAS
LOUISIANA
MISSISSIPPI
TENNESSEE
KENTUCKY
WEST VIRGINIA
VIRGINIA
ALABAMA
GEORGIA
SOUTH CAROLINA
NORTH CAROLINA
FLORIDA
PENNSYLVANIA
NEW YORK
VERMONT
NEW HAMPSHIRE
MAINE
MASSACHUSETTS
RHODE ISLAND
CONNECTICUT
NEW JERSEY
DELAWARE
MARYLAND

MEXICO

Miles
0   400

Each State has two Senators

Senators voting against the Treaty

Senators supporting the Treaty

Senators not voting

Despite Senate hostility to the Treaty,
President Wilson refused to re-write it.
Democrats who wanted changes joined
with Republicans who opposed the
Treaty altogether, and "unconditional
acceptance" was defeated on 19 November
1919 by 56 to 37 votes. Wilson attacked
"sullen and selfish isolation" in vain.
His successor, President Harding,
declared: "We seek no part in
directing the destinies of the world".
This was U.S. policy 1919-1939.

76

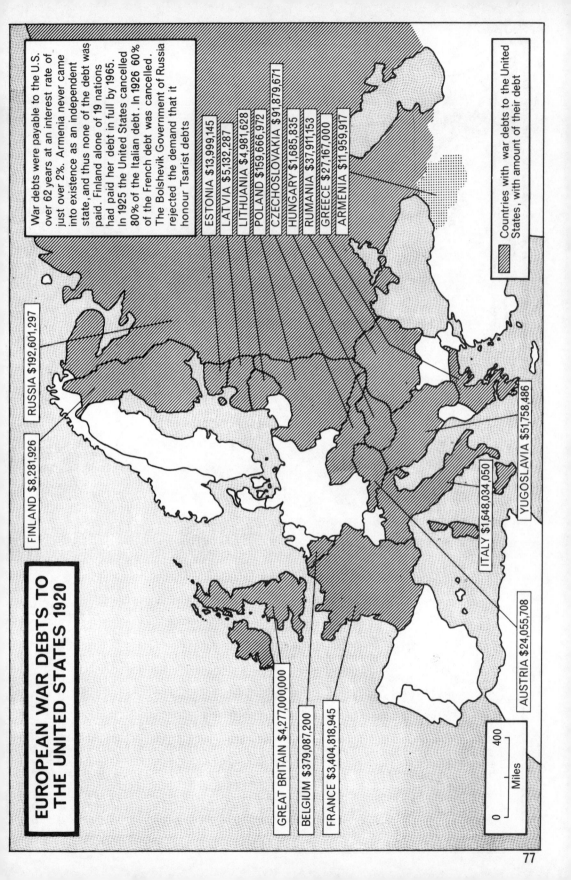

EUROPEAN WAR DEBTS TO THE UNITED STATES 1920

War debts were payable to the U.S. over 62 years at an interest rate of just over 2%. Armenia never came into existence as an independent state, and thus none of the debt was paid. Finland alone of 19 nations had paid her debt in full by 1965. In 1925 the United States cancelled 80% of the Italian debt. In 1926 60% of the French debt was cancelled. The Bolshevik Government of Russia rejected the demand that it honour Tsarist debts

ESTONIA $13,999,145
LATVIA $5,132,287
LITHUANIA $4,981,628
POLAND $159,666,972
CZECHOSLOVAKIA $91,879,671
HUNGARY $1,685,835
RUMANIA $37,911,153
GREECE $27,167,000
ARMENIA $11,959,917

Countries with war debts to the United States, with amount of their debt

FINLAND $192,601,297

RUSSIA $8,281,926

ITALY $1,648,034,050

YUGOSLAVIA $51,758,486

AUSTRIA $24,055,708

GREAT BRITAIN $4,277,000,000

BELGIUM $379,087,200

FRANCE $3,404,818,945

0   400
Miles

77

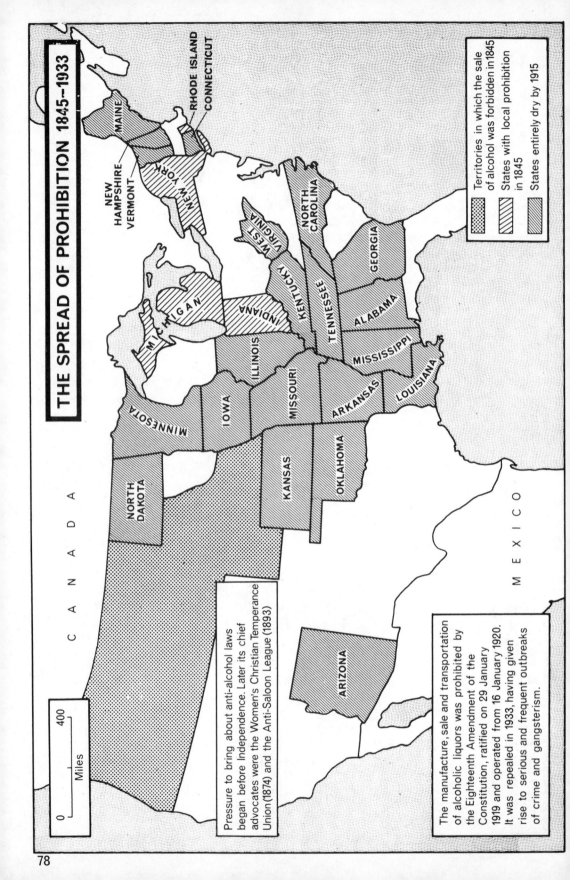

THE SPREAD OF PROHIBITION 1845—1933

CANADA

MEXICO

NEW HAMPSHIRE
VERMONT
MAINE
RHODE ISLAND
CONNECTICUT
NEW YORK
NORTH CAROLINA
GEORGIA
WEST VIRGINIA
KENTUCKY
TENNESSEE
ALABAMA
MICHIGAN
INDIANA
ILLINOIS
MISSISSIPPI
IOWA
MISSOURI
ARKANSAS
LOUISIANA
MINNESOTA
KANSAS
OKLAHOMA
NORTH DAKOTA
ARIZONA

Territories in which the sale
of alcohol was forbidden in 1845

States with local prohibition
in 1845

States entirely dry by 1915

0   400
Miles

Pressure to bring about anti-alcohol laws
began before Independence. Later its chief
advocates were the Women's Christian Temperance
Union (1874) and the Anti-Saloon League (1893)

The manufacture, sale and transportation
of alcoholic liquors was prohibited by
the Eighteenth Amendment of the
Constitution, ratified on 29 January
1919 and operated from 16 January 1920.
It was repealed in 1933, having given
rise to serious and frequent outbreaks
of crime and gangsterism.

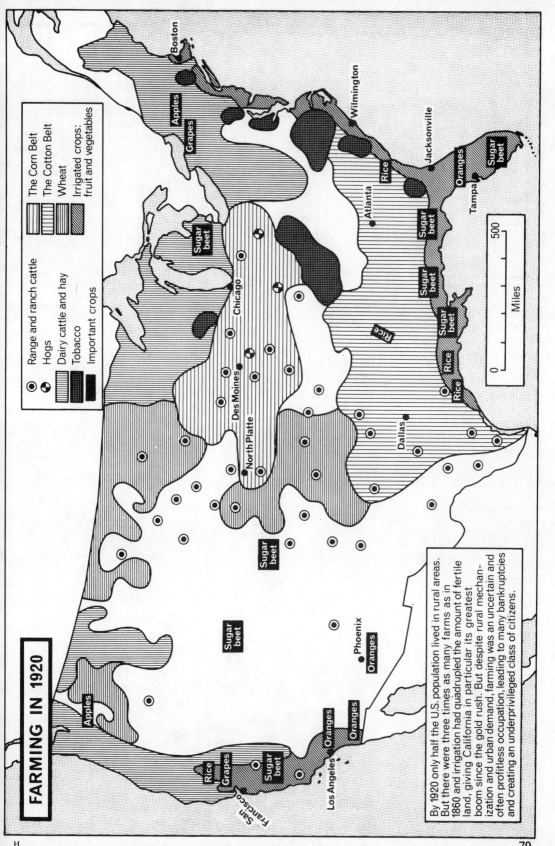

FARMING IN 1920

Legend:

Range and ranch cattle
Hogs
Dairy cattle and hay
Tobacco
Important crops

The Corn Belt
The Cotton Belt
Wheat
Irrigated crops: fruit and vegetables

Miles
0   500

By 1920 only half the U.S. population lived in rural areas. But there were three times as many farms as in 1860 and irrigation had quadrupled the amount of fertile land, giving California in particular its greatest boom since the gold rush. But despite rural mechanization and urban demand, farming was an uncertain and often profitless occupation, leading to many bankruptcies and creating an underprivileged class of citizens.

Map labels:

Boston
Apples
Grapes
Wilmington
Jacksonville
Sugar beet
Rice
Oranges
Tampa
Atlanta
Sugar beet
Sugar beet
Sugar beet
Rice
Rice
Rice
Chicago
Des Moines
North Platte
Dallas
Sugar beet
Sugar beet
Phoenix
Oranges
Apples
Rice
Grapes
Sugar beet
San Francisco
Los Angeles
Oranges
Oranges
Oranges

H

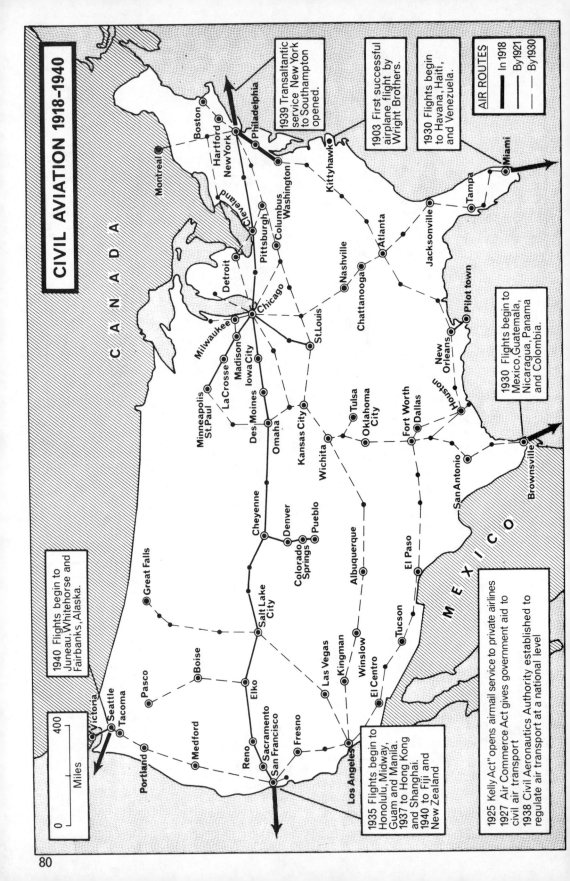

CIVIL AVIATION 1918–1940

AIR ROUTES
— In 1918
— By 1921
--- By 1930

CANADA

MEXICO

1939 Transatlantic service New York to Southampton opened.

1903 First successful airplane flight by Wright Brothers.

1930 Flights begin to Havana, Haiti, and Venezuela.

1930 Flights begin to Mexico, Guatemala, Nicaragua, Panama and Colombia.

1940 Flights begin to Juneau, Whitehorse and Fairbanks, Alaska.

1935 Flights begin to Honolulu, Midway, Guam and Manila. 1937 to Hong Kong and Shanghai. 1940 to Fiji and New Zealand

1925 Kelly Act" opens airmail service to private airlines
1927 Air Commerce Act gives government aid to civil air transport
1938 Civil Aeronautics Authority established to regulate air transport at a national level

400
0   Miles

Boston
Hartford
New York
Philadelphia
Montreal
Cleveland
Columbus
Washington
Kittyhawk
Miami
Tampa
Pittsburgh
Atlanta
Jacksonville
Detroit
Nashville
Chattanooga
Chicago
Pilot town
Milwaukee
Madison
Iowa City
St. Louis
New Orleans
La Crosse
Des Moines
Minneapolis St. Paul
Omaha
Kansas City
Wichita
Tulsa
Oklahoma City
Fort Worth
Dallas
Houston
Cheyenne
Denver
Pueblo
Colorado Springs
Albuquerque
El Paso
San Antonio
Brownsville
Great Falls
Salt Lake City
Las Vegas
Kingman
Winslow
Tucson
El Centro
Pasco
Boise
Elko
Reno
Sacramento
San Francisco
Fresno
Los Angeles
Medford
Portland
Seattle
Tacoma
Victoria

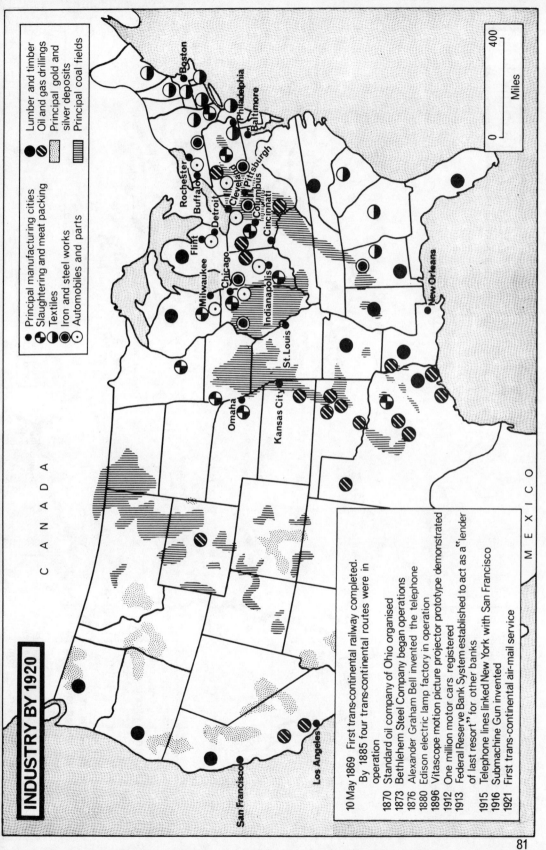

INDUSTRY BY 1920

Principal manufacturing cities
Slaughtering and meat packing
Textiles
Iron and steel works
Automobiles and parts

Lumber and timber
Oil and gas drillings
Principal gold and silver deposits
Principal coal fields

C A N A D A

M E X I C O

Boston
Philadelphia
Baltimore
Rochester
Buffalo
Cleveland
Pittsburgh
Detroit
Columbus
Cincinnati
Flint
Chicago
Milwaukee
Indianapolis
St. Louis
Omaha
Kansas City
New Orleans
San Francisco
Los Angeles

0   400
Miles

10 May 1869 First trans-continental railway completed.
             By 1885 four trans-continental routes were in
             operation
1870 Standard oil company of Ohio organised
1873 Bethlehem Steel Company began operations
1876 Alexander Graham Bell invented the telephone
1880 Edison electric lamp factory in operation
1896 Vitascope motion picture projector prototype demonstrated
1912 One million motor cars registered
1913 Federal Reserve Bank System established to act as a "lender
      of last resort" for other banks
1915 Telephone lines linked New York with San Francisco
1916 Submachine Gun invented
1921 First trans-continental air-mail service

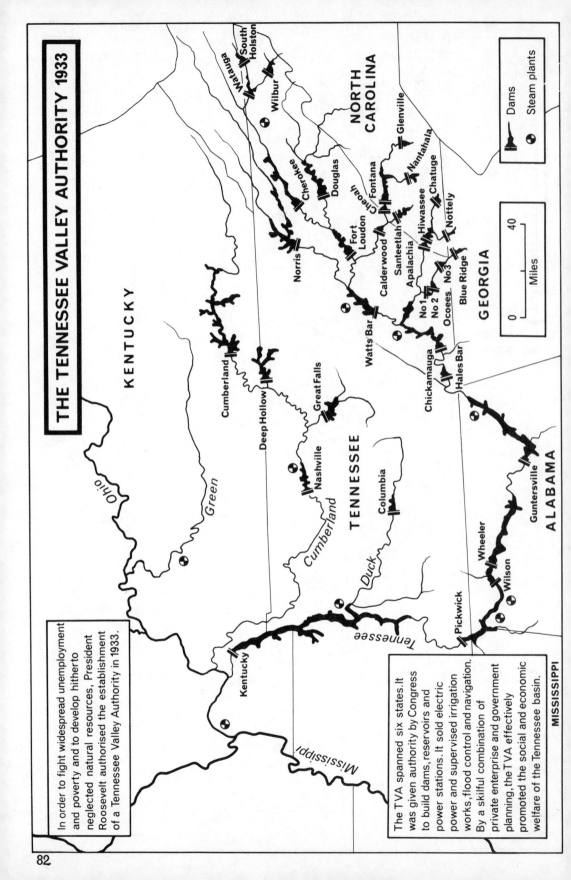

THE TENNESSEE VALLEY AUTHORITY 1933

In order to fight widespread unemployment and poverty and to develop hitherto neglected natural resources, President Roosevelt authorised the establishment of a Tennessee Valley Authority in 1933.

The TVA spanned six states. It was given authority by Congress to build dams, reservoirs and power stations. It sold electric power and supervised irrigation works, flood control and navigation. By a skilful combination of private enterprise and government planning, the TVA effectively promoted the social and economic welfare of the Tennessee basin.

Dams
Steam plants

Miles
0   40

KENTUCKY

NORTH CAROLINA

TENNESSEE

GEORGIA

ALABAMA

MISSISSIPPI

Ohio
Green
Cumberland
Duck
Tennessee
Mississippi

South Holston
Watauga
Wilbur
Cherokee
Douglas
Glenville
Nantahala
Cheoah
Fontana
Chatuge
Fort Loudon
Santeetlah
Hiwassee
Nottely
Norris
Calderwood
Apalachia
No 1
No 2
Ocoees No 3
Blue Ridge
Watts Bar
Chickamauga
Hales Bar
Cumberland
Deep Hollow
Great Falls
Nashville
Columbia
Kentucky
Pickwick
Wilson
Wheeler
Guntersville

82

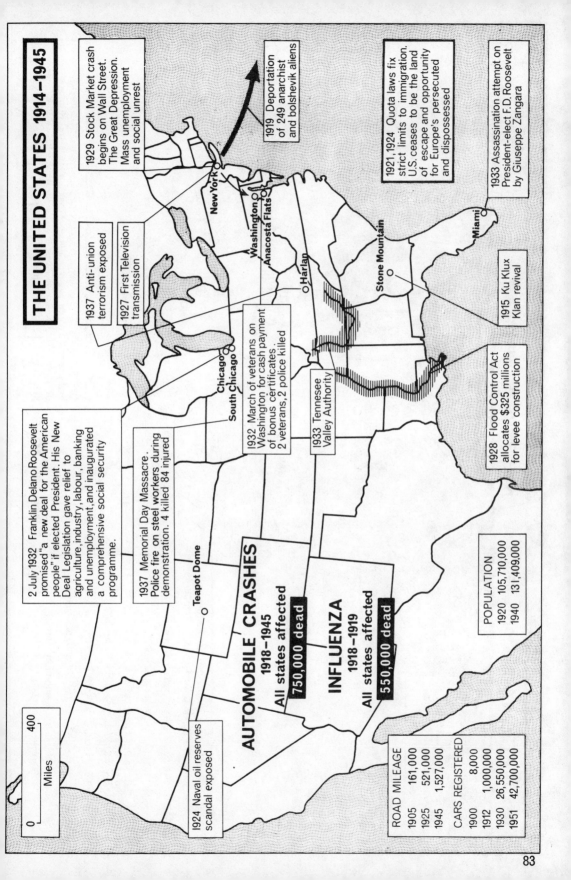

THE UNITED STATES 1914–1945

1929 Stock Market crash begins on Wall Street. The Great Depression. Mass unemployment and social unrest

1919 Deportation of 249 anarchist and bolshevik aliens

1921, 1924 Quota laws fix strict limits to immigration. U.S. ceases to be the land of escape and opportunity for Europe's persecuted and dispossessed

1933 Assassination attempt on President-elect F.D. Roosevelt by Giuseppe Zangara

1937 Anti-union terrorism exposed

1927 First Television transmission

New York

Washington
Anacosta Flats

Harlan

Stone Mountain

Miami

1915 Ku Klux Klan revival

2 July 1932 Franklin Delano Roosevelt promised "a new deal for the American people" if elected President. His New Deal Legislation gave relief to agriculture, industry, labour, banking and unemployment, and inaugurated a comprehensive social security programme.

1937 Memorial Day Massacre. Police fire on steel workers during demonstration. 4 killed 84 injured

1932 March of veterans on Washington for cash payment of bonus certificates. 2 veterans, 2 police killed

Chicago
South Chicago

1933 Tennesee Valley Authority

1928 Flood Control Act allocates $325 millions for levee construction

Teapot Dome

AUTOMOBILE CRASHES
1918–1945
All states affected

750,000 dead

INFLUENZA
1918–1919
All states affected

550,000 dead

1924 Naval oil reserves scandal exposed

POPULATION	
1920	105,710,000
1940	131,409,000

ROAD MILEAGE	
1905	161,000
1925	521,000
1945	1,527,000

CARS REGISTERED	
1900	8,000
1912	1,000,000
1930	26,550,000
1951	42,700,000

0	400
Miles	

83

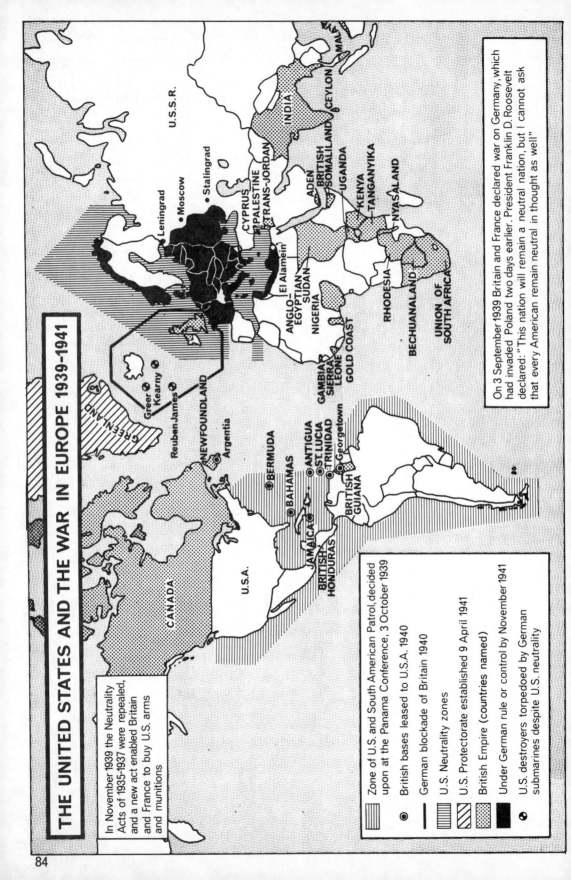

THE UNITED STATES AND THE WAR IN EUROPE 1939-1941

In November 1939 the Neutrality Acts of 1935-1937 were repealed, and a new act enabled Britain and France to buy U.S. arms and munitions

On 3 September 1939 Britain and France declared war on Germany, which had invaded Poland two days earlier. President Franklin D. Roosevelt declared: "This nation will remain a neutral nation, but I cannot ask that every American remain neutral in thought as well"

Legend:

Zone of U.S. and South American Patrol, decided upon at the Panama Conference, 3 October 1939

● British bases leased to U.S.A. 1940

| German blockade of Britain 1940

U.S. Neutrality zones

U.S. Protectorate established 9 April 1941

British Empire (countries named)

Under German rule or control by November 1941

✪ U.S. destroyers torpedoed by German submarines despite U.S. neutrality

Place labels on map:

U.S.S.R., Leningrad, Moscow, Stalingrad, CYPRUS, PALESTINE, TRANS-JORDAN, INDIA, CEYLON, ADEN, BRITISH SOMALILAND, UGANDA, KENYA, TANGANYIKA, NYASALAND, RHODESIA, BECHUANALAND, UNION OF SOUTH AFRICA, ANGLO-EGYPTIAN SUDAN, NIGERIA, GOLD COAST, GAMBIA, SIERRA LEONE, El Alamein, GREENLAND, Greer, Kearny, Reuben James, NEWFOUNDLAND, Argentia, CANADA, U.S.A., BERMUDA, BAHAMAS, JAMAICA, BRITISH HONDURAS, ANTIGUA, ST LUCIA, TRINIDAD, Georgetown, BRITISH GUIANA

84

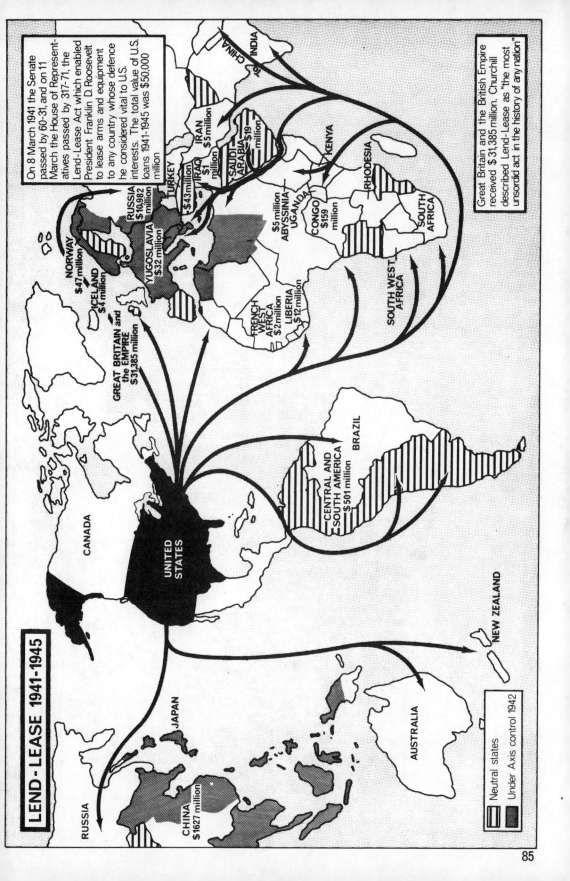

LEND-LEASE 1941-1945

On 8 March 1941 the Senate passed by 60-31, and on 11 March the House of Representatives passed by 317-71, the Lend-Lease Act which enabled President Franklin D Roosevelt to lease arms and equipment to any country whose defence he considered vital to U.S. interests. The total value of U.S. loans 1941-1945 was $50,000 million

Great Britain and the British Empire received $31,385 million. Churchill described Lend-Lease as "the most unsordid act in the history of any nation"

RUSSIA $10,982 million

NORWAY $47 million

ICELAND $4 million

YUGOSLAVIA $32 million

GREAT BRITAIN and the EMPIRE $31,385 million

TURKEY $43 million

IRAQ $1 million

IRAN $5 million

SAUDI-ARABIA $19 million

INDIA

CHINA

KENYA

ABYSSINIA $5 million

UGANDA

CONGO $159 million

RHODESIA

SOUTH AFRICA

SOUTH WEST AFRICA

FRENCH WEST AFRICA $2 million

LIBERIA $12 million

CANADA

UNITED STATES

CENTRAL AND SOUTH AMERICA $501 million

BRAZIL

RUSSIA

JAPAN

CHINA $1627 million

AUSTRALIA

NEW ZEALAND

Neutral states

Under Axis control 1942

85

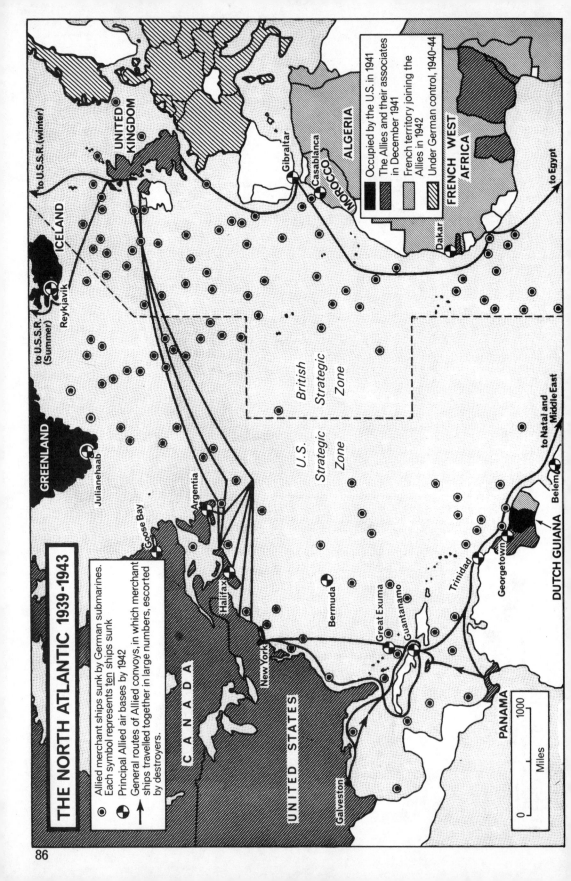

THE NORTH ATLANTIC 1939-1943

⊙ Allied merchant ships sunk by German submarines.
Each symbol represents ten ships sunk

◕ Principal Allied air bases by 1942

↑ General routes of Allied convoys, in which merchant ships travelled together in large numbers, escorted by destroyers.

Occupied by the U.S. in 1941

The Allies and their associates in December 1941

French territory joining the Allies in 1942

Under German control, 1940-44

GREENLAND

ICELAND

UNITED KINGDOM

to U.S.S.R. (winter)

to U.S.S.R. (Summer)

Reykjavik

Julianehaab

Goose Bay

Argentia

Halifax

CANADA

UNITED STATES

New York

Galveston

PANAMA

Bermuda

Great Exuma

Guantanamo

Trinidad

Georgetown

DUTCH GUIANA

Belem

to Natal and Middle East

British Strategic Zone

U.S. Strategic Zone

Gibraltar

Casablanca

MOROCCO

ALGERIA

Dakar

FRENCH WEST AFRICA

to Egypt

0   1000
Miles

86

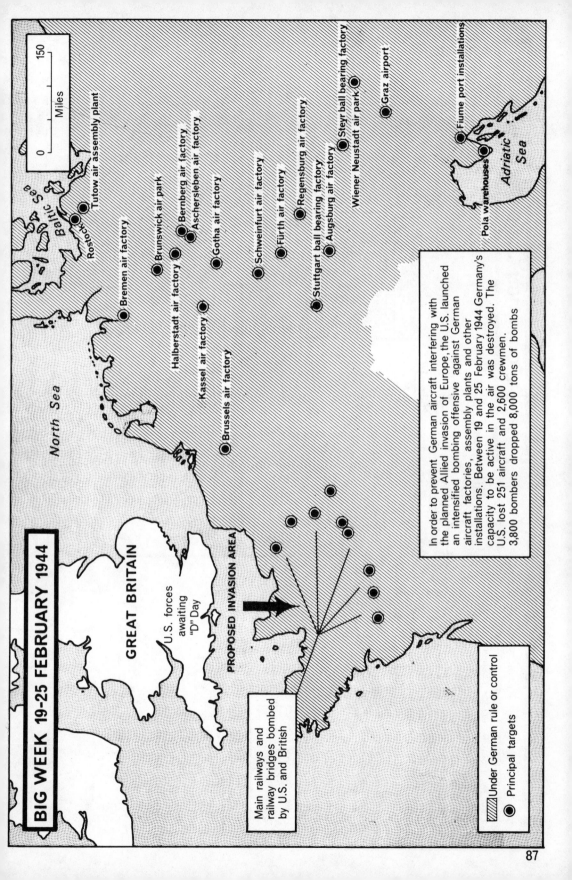

BIG WEEK 19-25 FEBRUARY 1944

GREAT BRITAIN

U.S. forces awaiting "D" Day

PROPOSED INVASION AREA

Main railways and railway bridges bombed by U.S. and British

North Sea

Baltic Sea

Rostock

Tutow air assembly plant

Bremen air factory

Brunswick air park

Bernberg air factory

Aschersleben air factory

Halberstadt air factory

Gotha air factory

Kassel air factory

Brussels air factory

Schweinfurt air factory

Fürth air factory

Regensburg air factory

Stuttgart ball bearing factory

Augsburg air factory

Steyr ball bearing factory

Wiener Neustadt air park

Graz airport

Pola warehouses

Fiume port installations

Adriatic Sea

Miles
0   150

In order to prevent German aircraft interfering with the planned Allied invasion of Europe, the U.S. launched an intensified bombing offensive against German aircraft factories, assembly plants and other installations. Between 19 and 25 February 1944 Germany's capacity to be active in the air was destroyed. The U.S. lost 251 aircraft and 2,600 crewmen. The 3,800 bombers dropped 8,000 tons of bombs.

Under German rule or control

Principal targets

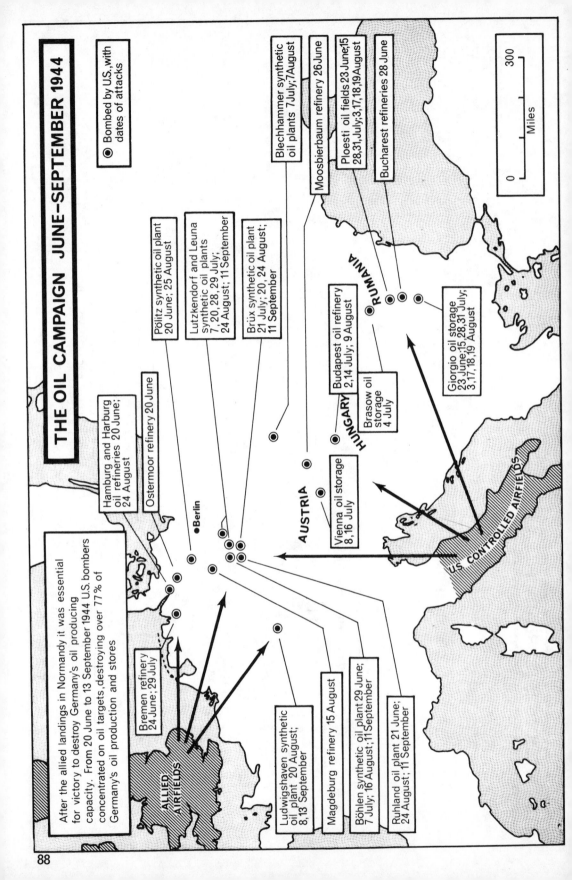

THE OIL CAMPAIGN JUNE–SEPTEMBER 1944

⊙ Bombed by U.S.,with dates of attacks

After the allied landings in Normandy it was essential for victory to destroy Germany's oil producing capacity. From 20 June to 13 September 1944 U.S. bombers concentrated on oil targets, destroying over 77% of Germany's oil production and stores

Blechhammer synthetic oil plants 7 July; 7August

Moosbierbaum refinery 26June

Ploesti oil fields 23June;15 28,31July;3,17,18,19August

Bucharest refineries 28 June

Pölitz synthetic oil plant 20 June; 25 August

Lutzkendorf and Leuna synthetic oil plants 7, 20, 28, 29 July; 24 August; 11 September

Brüx synthetic oil plant 21 July; 20, 24 August; 11 September

Budapest oil refinery 2, 14 July; 9 August

Giorgio oil storage 23 June;15,28,31 July; 3, 17, 18, 19 August

Hamburg and Harburg oil refineries 20 June; 24 August

Ostermoor refinery 20 June

Brasow oil storage 4 July

Vienna oil storage 8,16 July

RUMANIA

HUNGARY

AUSTRIA

•Berlin

US CONTROLLED AIRFIELDS

ALLIED AIRFIELDS

Bremen refinery 24 June; 29 July

Ludwigshaven synthetic oil plant 20 August; 8,13 September

Magdeburg refinery 15 August

Böhlen synthetic oil plant 29 June; 7 July; 16 August;11September

Ruhland oil plant 21 June; 24 August; 11 September

Miles

0   300

88

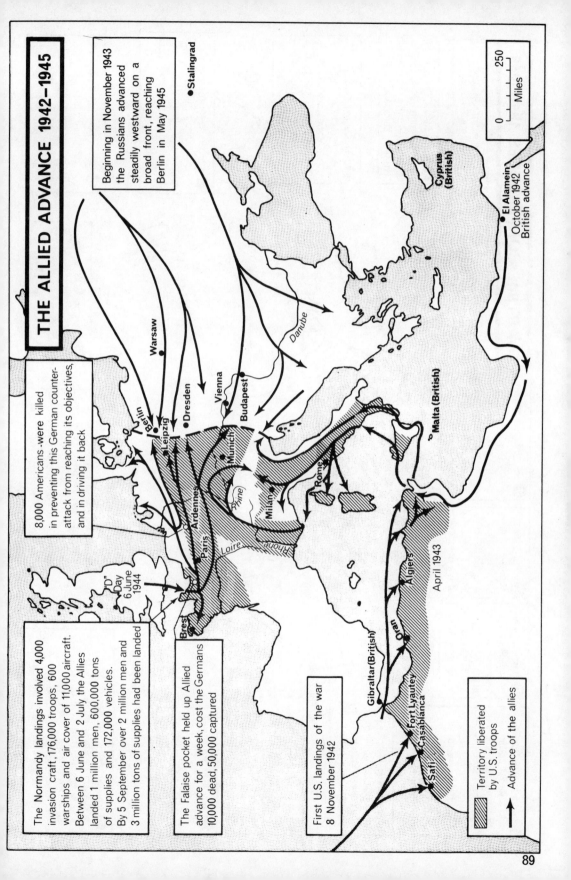

THE ALLIED ADVANCE 1942–1945

Beginning in November 1943 the Russians advanced steadily westward on a broad front, reaching Berlin in May 1945

•Stalingrad

0   250
Miles

Cyprus (British)

•El Alamein
October 1942
British advance

Warsaw

Danube

Malta (British)

8,000 Americans were killed in preventing this German counter-attack from reaching its objectives, and in driving it back

Berlin
Leipzig •Dresden
Vienna
Budapest
Munich
Rome
Milan
Rhine
Ardennes
Paris
Loire
Rhône

The Normandy landings involved 4,000 invasion craft, 176,000 troops, 600 warships and air cover of 11,000 aircraft. Between 6 June and 2 July the Allies landed 1 million men, 600,000 tons of supplies and 172,000 vehicles. By 5 September over 2 million men and 3 million tons of supplies had been landed

"D" Day 6 June 1944

Brest

The Falaise pocket held up Allied advance for a week, cost the Germans 10,000 dead, 50,000 captured

April 1943

Algiers

First U.S. landings of the war 8 November 1942

Gibraltar(British)
Oran
Fort Lyautey
Casablanca
Safi

Territory liberated by U.S. troops

Advance of the allies

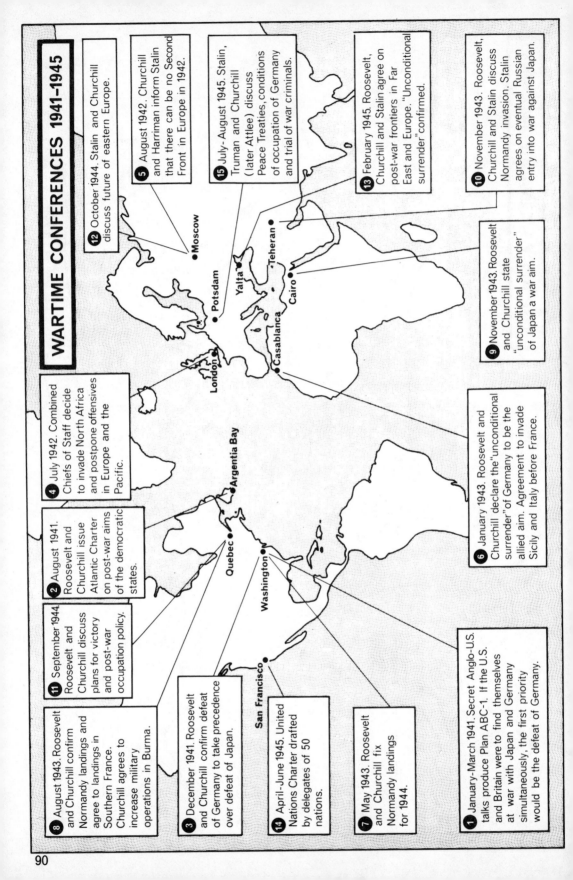

WARTIME CONFERENCES 1941-1945

12 October 1944. Stalin and Churchill discuss future of eastern Europe.

5 August 1942. Churchill and Harriman inform Stalin that there can be no Second Front in Europe in 1942.

15 July–August 1945. Stalin, Truman and Churchill (later Attlee) discuss Peace Treaties, conditions of occupation of Germany and trial of war criminals.

13 February 1945. Stalin, Churchill and Stalin agree on post-war frontiers in Far East and Europe. "Unconditional surrender" confirmed.

10 November 1943. Roosevelt, Churchill and Stalin discuss Normandy invasion. Stalin agrees on eventual Russian entry into war against Japan.

4 July 1942. Combined Chiefs of Staff decide to invade North Africa and postpone offensives in Europe and the Pacific.

2 August 1941. Roosevelt and Churchill issue Atlantic Charter on post-war aims of the democratic states.

11 September 1944. Roosevelt and Churchill discuss plans for victory and post-war occupation policy.

9 November 1943. Roosevelt and Churchill state "unconditional surrender" of Japan as a war aim.

6 January 1943. Roosevelt and Churchill declare the "unconditional surrender" of Germany to be the allied aim. Agreement to invade Sicily and Italy before France.

8 August 1943. Roosevelt and Churchill confirm Normandy landings and agree to landings in Southern France. Churchill agrees to increase military operations in Burma.

3 December 1941. Roosevelt and Churchill confirm defeat of Germany to take precedence over defeat of Japan.

14 April–June 1945. United Nations Charter drafted by delegates of 50 nations.

7 May 1943. Roosevelt and Churchill fix Normandy landings for 1944.

1 January–March 1941. Secret Anglo-U.S. talks produce Plan ABC-1. If the U.S. and Britain were to find themselves at war with Japan and Germany simultaneously, the first priority would be the defeat of Germany.

Moscow

Potsdam

Yalta

Teheran

Cairo

Casablanca

London

Argentia Bay

Quebec

Washington

San Francisco

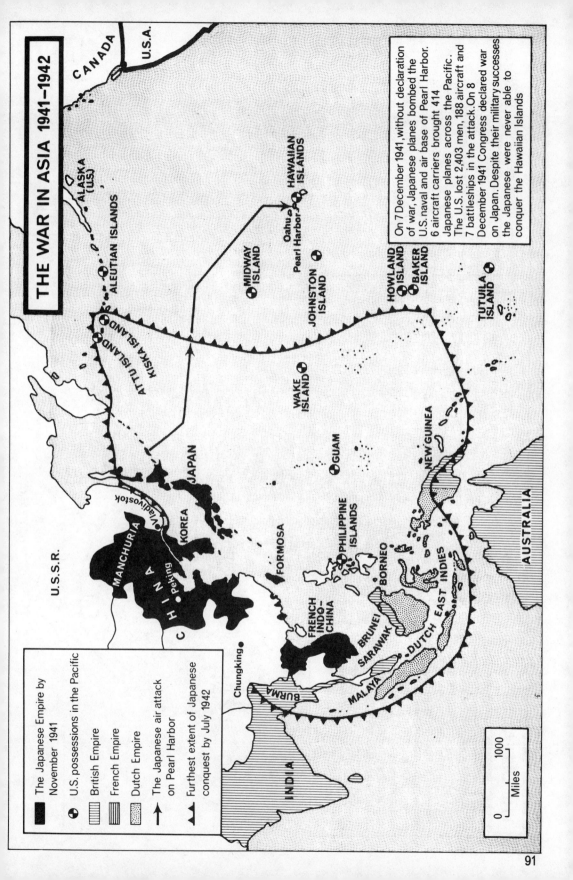

THE WAR IN ASIA 1941-1942

On 7 December 1941, without declaration of war, Japanese planes bombed the U.S. naval and air base of Pearl Harbor. 6 aircraft carriers brought 414 Japanese planes across the Pacific. The U.S. lost 2,403 men, 188 aircraft and 7 battleships in the attack. On 8 December 1941 Congress declared war on Japan. Despite their military successes the Japanese were never able to conquer the Hawaiian Islands

CANADA
U.S.A.
ALASKA (U.S.)
ALEUTIAN ISLANDS
ATTU ISLAND
KISKA ISLAND
U.S.S.R.
Vladivostok
MANCHURIA
KOREA
JAPAN
Peking
C H I N A
Chungking
FORMOSA
FRENCH INDO-CHINA
BURMA
INDIA
MALAYA
BRUNEI
SARAWAK
BORNEO
DUTCH EAST INDIES
PHILIPPINE ISLANDS
GUAM
WAKE ISLAND
NEW GUINEA
AUSTRALIA
MIDWAY ISLAND
Oahu
Pearl Harbor
HAWAIIAN ISLANDS
JOHNSTON ISLAND
HOWLAND ISLAND
BAKER ISLAND
TUTUILA ISLAND

Legend:
- The Japanese Empire by November 1941
- ⊕ U.S. possessions in the Pacific
- British Empire
- French Empire
- Dutch Empire
- ↑ The Japanese air attack on Pearl Harbor
- ▲▲ Furthest extent of Japanese conquest by July 1942

0   1000
Miles

91

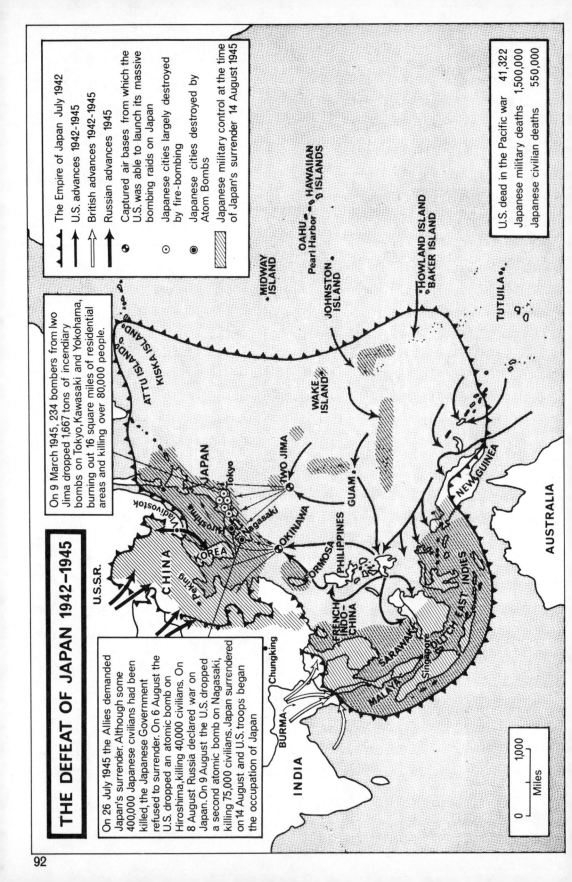

THE DEFEAT OF JAPAN 1942–1945

On 26 July 1945 the Allies demanded Japan's surrender. Although some 400,000 Japanese civilians had been killed, the Japanese Government refused to surrender. On 6 August the U.S. dropped an atomic bomb on Hiroshima, killing 40,000 civilians. On 8 August Russia declared war on Japan. On 9 August the U.S. dropped a second atomic bomb on Nagasaki, killing 75,000 civilians. Japan surrendered on 14 August and U.S. troops began the occupation of Japan

On 9 March 1945, 234 bombers from Iwo Jima dropped 1,667 tons of incendiary bombs on Tokyo, Kawasaki and Yokohama, burning out 16 square miles of residential areas and killing over 80,000 people.

The Empire of Japan July 1942

U.S. advances 1942–1945

British advances 1942–1945

Russian advances 1945

Captured air bases from which the U.S. was able to launch its massive bombing raids on Japan

⊙ Japanese cities largely destroyed by fire-bombing

● Japanese cities destroyed by Atom Bombs

Japanese military control at the time of Japan's surrender 14 August 1945

U.S. dead in the Pacific war	41,322
Japanese military deaths	1,500,000
Japanese civilian deaths	550,000

0   1,000

Miles

INDIA

BURMA

Chungking

CHINA

Peking

U.S.S.R.

Vladivostok

KOREA

JAPAN

Tokyo

Hiroshima

Nagasaki

OKINAWA

IWO JIMA

FORMOSA

PHILIPPINES

GUAM

FRENCH INDO-CHINA

MALAYA

Singapore

SARAWAK

DUTCH EAST INDIES

NEW GUINEA

AUSTRALIA

ATTU ISLAND

KISKA ISLAND

MIDWAY ISLAND

OAHU

Pearl Harbor

HAWAIIAN ISLANDS

JOHNSTON ISLAND

WAKE ISLAND

HOWLAND ISLAND

BAKER ISLAND

TUTUILA

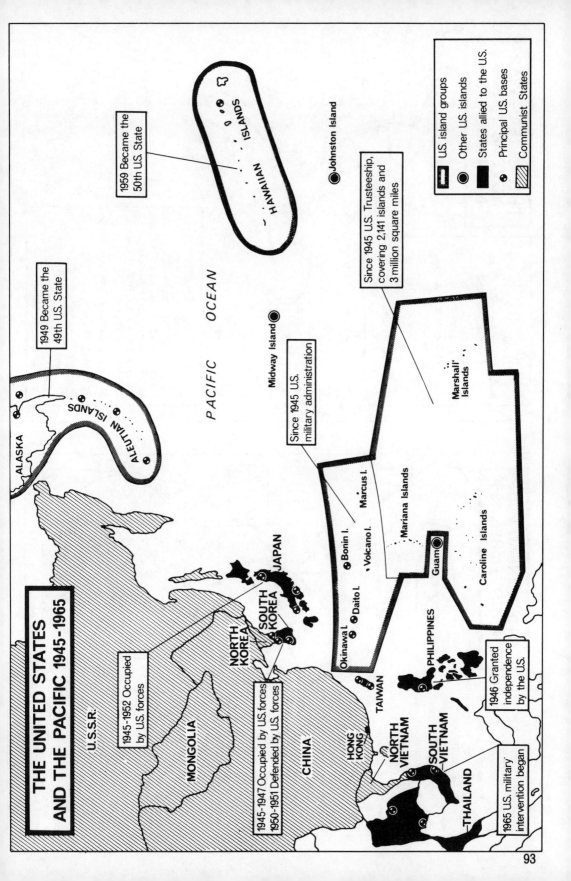

THE UNITED STATES
AND THE PACIFIC 1945-1965

U.S.S.R.

ALASKA

1949 Became the 49th U.S. State

ALEUTIAN ISLANDS

PACIFIC OCEAN

Midway Island ●

1959 Became the 50th U.S. State

HAWAIIAN ISLANDS

Johnston Island ●

Since 1945 U.S. Trusteeship, covering 2,141 islands and 3 million square miles

Since 1945 U.S. military administration

Marcus I.

Bonin I. ⊕
Volcano I. ⊕

Mariana Islands

Marshall Islands

MONGOLIA

CHINA

1945-1952 Occupied by U.S. forces

NORTH KOREA

SOUTH KOREA

JAPAN

1945-1947 Occupied by U.S. forces
1950-1951 Defended by U.S. forces

Okinawa I. ⊕
Daito I. ⊕

Guam ◉

Caroline Islands

HONG KONG

TAIWAN

PHILIPPINES

1946 Granted independence by the U.S.

NORTH VIETNAM

THAILAND

SOUTH VIETNAM

1965 U.S. military intervention began

Legend:
⬜ U.S. island groups
◉ Other U.S. islands
⬛ States allied to the U.S.
⊕ Principal U.S. bases
▨ Communist States

93

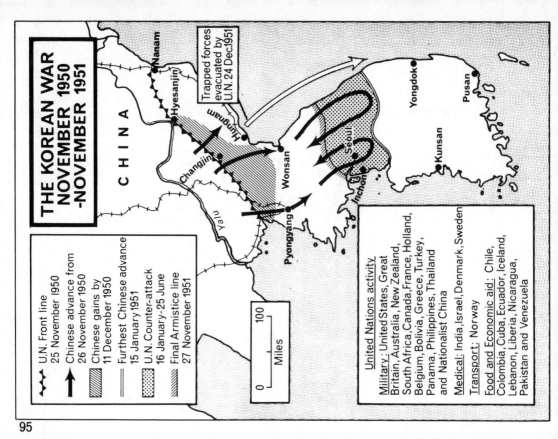

THE KOREAN WAR NOVEMBER 1950 -NOVEMBER 1951

Trapped forces evacuated by U.N. 24 Dec.1951

Legend:

- ⌇⌇⌇ U.N. Front line 25 November 1950
- ➤ Chinese advance from 26 November 1950
- ▨ Chinese gains by 11 December 1950
- ≡ Furthest Chinese advance 15 January 1951
- ▦ U.N. Counter-attack 16 January-25 June
- ▨ Final Armistice line 27 November 1951

Miles 0 ___ 100

United Nations activity

Military: United States, Great Britain, Australia, New Zealand, South Africa, Canada, France, Holland, Belgium, Bolivia, Greece, Turkey, Panama, Philippines, Thailand and Nationalist China

Medical: India, Israel, Denmark, Sweden

Transport: Norway

Food and Economic aid: Chile, Colombia, Cuba, Ecuador, Iceland, Lebanon, Liberia, Nicaragua, Pakistan and Venezuela

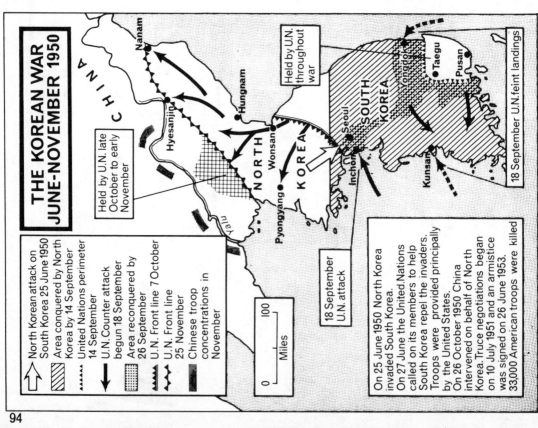

THE KOREAN WAR JUNE-NOVEMBER 1950

Held by U.N. late October to early November

Held by U.N. throughout war

18 September U.N. feint landings

18 September U.N. attack

Legend:

- ⇧ North Korean attack on South Korea 25 June 1950
- ▨ Area conquered by North Korea by 14 September
- ▪▪▪▪ United Nations perimeter 14 September
- ➤ U.N. Counter attack begun 18 September
- ▦ Area reconquered by 26 September
- ◤◤◤ U.N. Front line 7 October
- ⌇⌇⌇ U.N. Front line 25 November
- ▮ Chinese troop concentrations in November

Miles 0 ___ 100

On 25 June 1950 North Korea invaded South Korea.
On 27 June the United Nations called on its members to help South Korea repel the invaders. Troops were provided principally by the United States.
On 26 October 1950 China intervened on behalf of North Korea. Truce negotiations began on 10 July 1951 and an armistice was signed on 26 June 1953. 33,000 American troops were killed

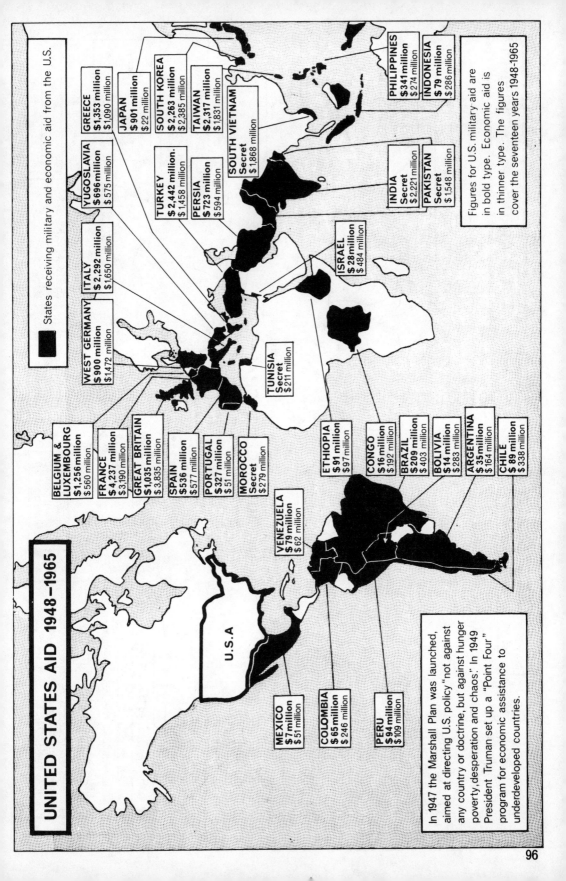

UNITED STATES AID 1948–1965

■ States receiving military and economic aid from the U.S.

Figures for U.S. military aid are in bold type. Economic aid is in thinner type. The figures cover the seventeen years 1948-1965.

GREECE $1,353 million $1,090 million

JAPAN $901 million $22 million

SOUTH KOREA $2,263 million $2,385 million

TAIWAN $2,317 million $1,831 million

SOUTH VIETNAM Secret $1,868 million

PHILIPPINES $341 million $274 million

INDONESIA $79 million $286 million

YUGOSLAVIA $696 million $575 million

TURKEY $2,442 million. $1,458 million

PERSIA $723 million $594 million

INDIA Secret $2,221 million

PAKISTAN Secret $1,548 million

ITALY $2,292 million $1,650 million

ISRAEL $28 million $484 million

WEST GERMANY $900 million $1,472 million

TUNISIA Secret $211 million

BELGIUM & LUXEMBOURG $1,256 million $560 million

FRANCE $4,237 million $3,190 million

GREAT BRITAIN $1,035 million $3,835 million

SPAIN $536 million $577 million

PORTUGAL $327 million $51 million

MOROCCO Secret $279 million

ETHIOPIA $91 million $97 million

CONGO $16 million $192 million

BRAZIL $209 million $403 million

BOLIVIA $14 million $283 million

ARGENTINA $35 million $164 million

CHILE $89 million $338 million

VENEZUELA $79 million $62 million

U.S.A

MEXICO $7 million $51 million

COLOMBIA $65 million $246 million

PERU $94 million $109 million

In 1947 the Marshall Plan was launched, aimed at directing U.S. policy "not against any country or doctrine, but against hunger poverty, desperation and chaos". In 1949 President Truman set up a "Point Four" program for economic assistance to underdeveloped countries.

96

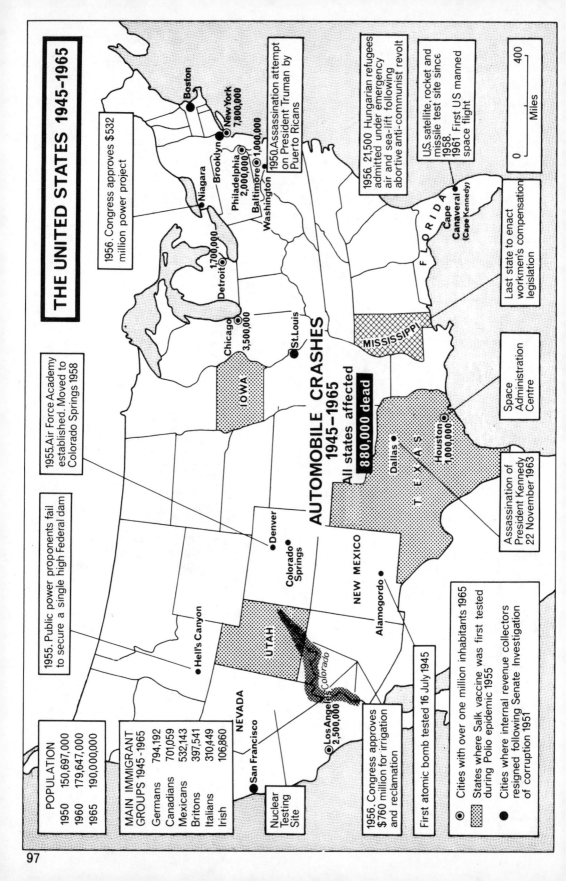

THE UNITED STATES 1945–1965

1956. Congress approves $532 million power project

1950. Assassination attempt on President Truman by Puerto Ricans

1956. 21,500 Hungarian refugees admitted under emergency air and sea-lift following abortive anti-communist revolt

U.S. satellite, rocket and missile test site since 1958.
1961. First US manned space flight

Last state to enact workmen's compensation legislation

Space Administration Centre

Assassination of President Kennedy 22 November 1963

1955. Air Force Academy established. Moved to Colorado Springs 1958

1955. Public power proponents fail to secure a single high Federal dam

1956. Congress approves $760 million for irrigation and reclamation

First atomic bomb tested 16 July 1945

⊙ Cities with over one million inhabitants 1965

▨ States where Salk vaccine was first tested during Polio epidemic 1955

● Cities where internal revenue collectors resigned following Senate Investigation of corruption 1951

POPULATION

1950	150,697,000
1960	179,647,000
1965	190,000,000

MAIN IMMIGRANT GROUPS 1945–1965

Germans	794,192
Canadians	701,059
Mexicans	532,143
Britons	397,541
Italians	310,449
Irish	106,860

Nuclear Testing Site

AUTOMOBILE CRASHES 1945–1965

All states affected

880,000 dead

Boston

New York 7,800,000

Brooklyn

Niagara

Philadelphia 2,000,000

Baltimore 1,000,000

Washington

Detroit 1,700,000

Chicago 3,500,000

St.Louis

FLORIDA

Cape Canaveral (Cape Kennedy)

MISSISSIPPI

IOWA

Dallas

Houston 1,000,000

TEXAS

NEW MEXICO

Alamogordo

Denver

Colorado Springs

Hell's Canyon

UTAH

Colorado

NEVADA

San Francisco

Los Angeles 2,500,000

0				400

Miles

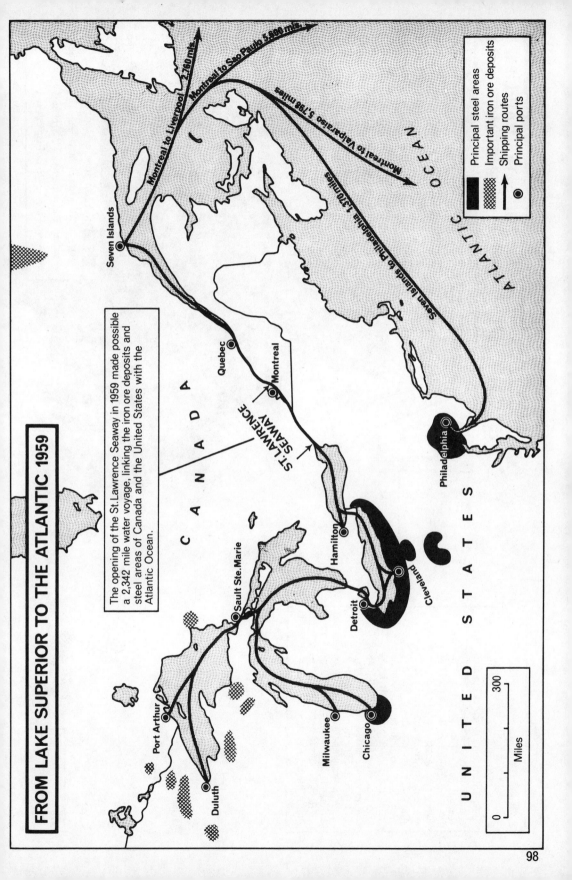

FROM LAKE SUPERIOR TO THE ATLANTIC 1959

The opening of the St.Lawrence Seaway in 1959 made possible a 2,342 mile water voyage, linking the iron ore deposits and steel areas of Canada and the United States with the Atlantic Ocean.

Legend:
- Principal steel areas
- Important iron ore deposits
- Shipping routes
- Principal ports

Montreal to Liverpool 2,760 mls.

Montreal to Sao Paulo 5,600 mls.

Montreal to Valparaiso 5,198 miles

Seven Islands to Philadelphia 1,370 miles

ATLANTIC OCEAN

Seven Islands

Quebec

Montreal

ST.LAWRENCE SEAWAY

Philadelphia

Hamilton

Cleveland

Detroit

Sault Ste.Marie

CANADA

Port Arthur

Duluth

Milwaukee

Chicago

UNITED STATES

0   300
Miles

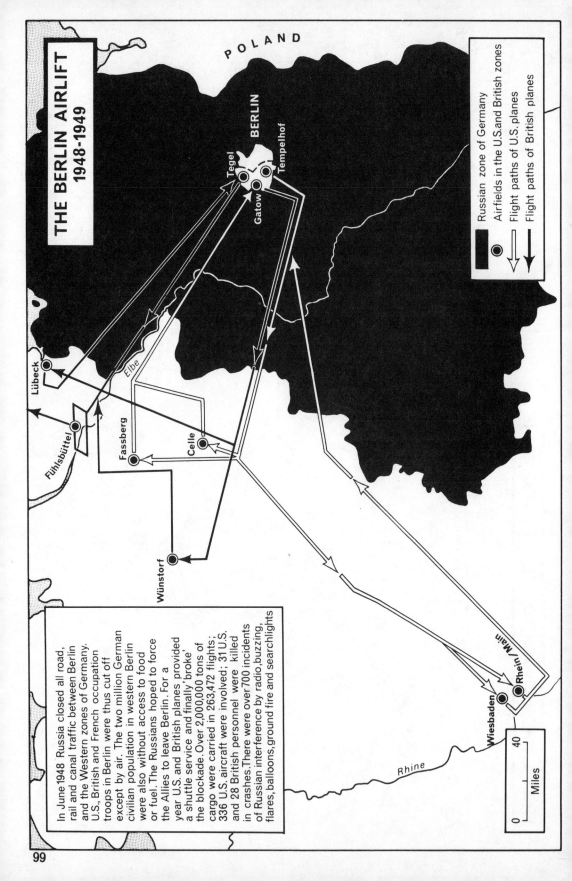

THE BERLIN AIRLIFT
1948-1949

POLAND

BERLIN

Tegel
Gatow
Tempelhof

Lübeck

Elbe

Fühlsbüttel

Fassberg

Celle

Wünstorf

Wiesbaden

Rhein/Main

Rhine

Legend:

Russian zone of Germany

Airfields in the U.S. and British zones

Flight paths of U.S. planes

Flight paths of British planes

0   40
Miles

In June 1948 Russia closed all road, rail and canal traffic between Berlin and the Western zones of Germany. U.S., British and French occupation troops in Berlin were thus cut off except by air. The two million German civilian population in western Berlin were also without access to food or fuel. The Russians hoped to force the Allies to leave Berlin. For a year U.S. and British planes provided a shuttle service and finally 'broke' the blockade. Over 2,000,000 tons of cargo were carried in 263,472 flights; 336 U.S. aircraft were involved; 31 U.S. and 28 British personnel were killed in crashes. There were over 700 incidents of Russian interference by radio, buzzing, flares, balloons, ground fire and searchlights

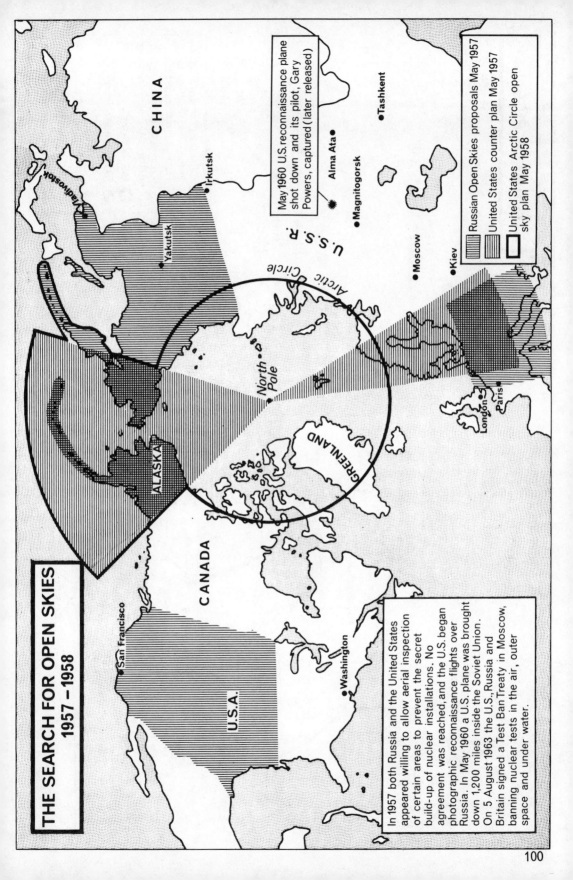

THE SEARCH FOR OPEN SKIES
1957 – 1958

CHINA

U.S.S.R.

Vladivostok

Irkutsk

Yakutsk

Alma Ata

Magnitogorsk

Tashkent

Moscow

Kiev

May 1960 U.S. reconnaissance plane shot down and its pilot, Gary Powers, captured (later released)

Arctic Circle

North Pole

GREENLAND

London

Paris

ALASKA

CANADA

U.S.A.

San Francisco

Washington

Russian Open Skies proposals May 1957

United States counter plan May 1957

United States Arctic Circle open sky plan May 1958

In 1957 both Russia and the United States appeared willing to allow aerial inspection of certain areas to prevent the secret build-up of nuclear installations. No agreement was reached, and the U.S. began photographic reconnaissance flights over Russia. In May 1960 a U.S. plane was brought down 1,200 miles inside the Soviet Union. On 5 August 1963 the U.S., Russia and Britain signed a Test Ban Treaty in Moscow, banning nuclear tests in the air, outer space and under water.

100

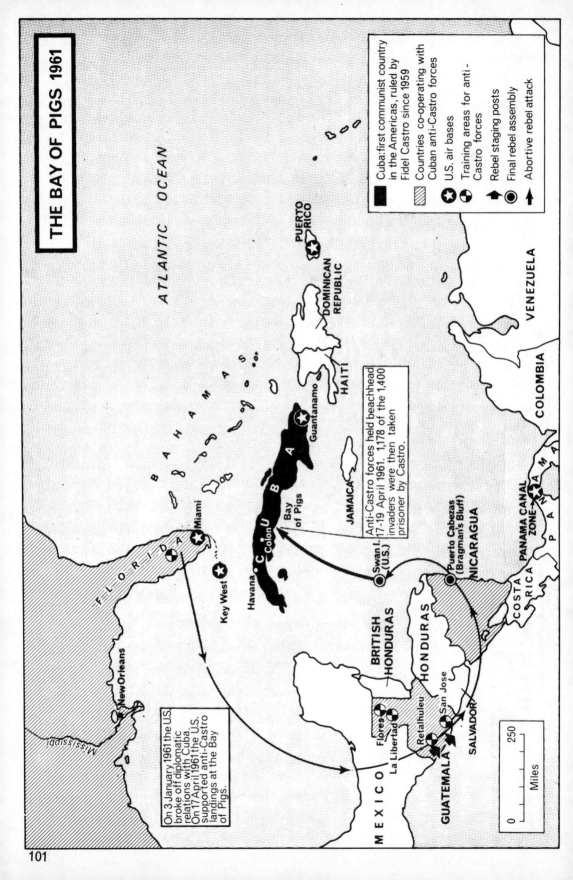

THE BAY OF PIGS 1961

ATLANTIC OCEAN

Legend:
- ▪ Cuba: first communist country in the Americas, ruled by Fidel Castro since 1959
- ▨ Countries co-operating with Cuban anti-Castro forces
- ✪ U.S. air bases
- ◒ Training areas for anti-Castro forces
- ⬆ Rebel staging posts
- ◉ Final rebel assembly
- ↑ Abortive rebel attack

PUERTO RICO

DOMINICAN REPUBLIC

HAITI

B A H A M A S

Miami

FLORIDA

Key West

New Orleans

Mississippi

M E X I C O

Havana · C U B A
Colon
Bay of Pigs
Guantanamo

JAMAICA

Anti-Castro forces held beachhead 17-19 April 1961. 1,178 of the 1,400 invaders were then taken prisoner by Castro.

Swan I. (U.S.)

BRITISH HONDURAS

Flores
La Libertad

Retalhuleu
San Jose
GUATEMALA
SALVADOR

HONDURAS

Puerto Cabezas (Bragman's Bluff)

NICARAGUA

COSTA RICA

PANAMA CANAL ZONE

P A N A M A

COLOMBIA

VENEZUELA

On 3 January 1961 the U.S. broke off diplomatic relations with Cuba. On 17 April 1961 the U.S. supported anti-Castro landings at the Bay of Pigs.

0   250
|————————|
Miles

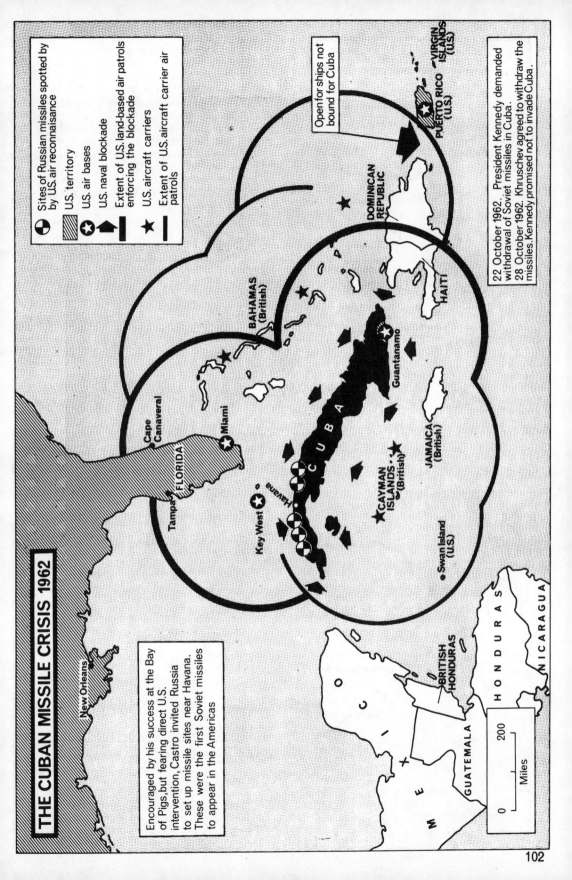

THE CUBAN MISSILE CRISIS 1962

Encouraged by his success at the Bay of Pigs, but fearing direct U.S. intervention, Castro invited Russia to set up missile sites near Havana. These were the first Soviet missiles to appear in the Americas

Legend:

- ◑ Sites of Russian missiles spotted by U.S. air reconnaissance
- ▨ U.S. territory
- ✪ U.S. air bases
- ⬛ U.S. naval blockade
- — Extent of U.S. land-based air patrols enforcing the blockade
- ★ U.S. aircraft carriers
- — Extent of U.S. aircraft carrier air patrols

Open for ships not bound for Cuba

22 October 1962. President Kennedy demanded withdrawal of Soviet missiles in Cuba.
28 October 1962. Khruschev agreed to withdraw the missiles. Kennedy promised not to invade Cuba.

New Orleans

Tampa

FLORIDA

Cape Canaveral

Miami

Key West

Havana

C U B A

Guantanamo

BAHAMAS (British)

CAYMAN ISLANDS (British)

JAMAICA (British)

Swan Island (U.S.)

HAITI

DOMINICAN REPUBLIC

PUERTO RICO (U.S.)

VIRGIN ISLANDS (U.S.)

MEXICO

GUATEMALA

BRITISH HONDURAS

H O N D U R A S

N I C A R A G U A

0   200
Miles

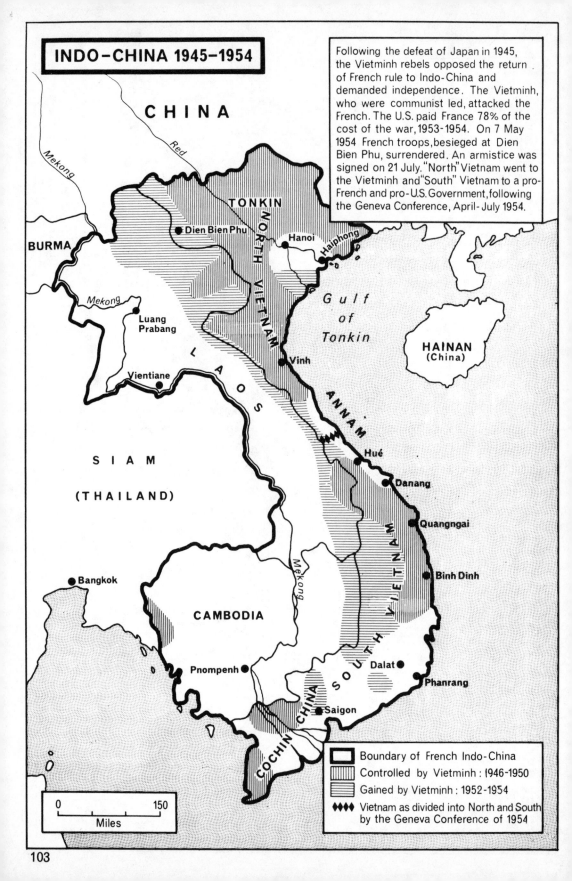

INDO-CHINA 1945-1954

Following the defeat of Japan in 1945, the Vietminh rebels opposed the return of French rule to Indo-China and demanded independence. The Vietminh, who were communist led, attacked the French. The U.S. paid France 78% of the cost of the war, 1953-1954. On 7 May 1954 French troops, besieged at Dien Bien Phu, surrendered. An armistice was signed on 21 July. "North" Vietnam went to the Vietminh and "South" Vietnam to a pro-French and pro-U.S. Government, following the Geneva Conference, April-July 1954.

CHINA

Mekong

Red

TONKIN

Dien Bien Phu

Hanoi

Haiphong

NORTH VIETNAM

BURMA

Mekong

Luang Prabang

Gulf
of
Tonkin

HAINAN
(China)

LAOS

Vientiane

Vinh

ANNAM

Hué

SIAM

(THAILAND)

Danang

Quangngai

SOUTH VIETNAM

Bangkok

Mekong

Binh Dinh

CAMBODIA

Pnompenh

Dalat

Phanrang

COCHIN CHINA

Saigon

Boundary of French Indo-China

Controlled by Vietminh : 1946-1950

Gained by Vietminh : 1952-1954

◆◆◆◆ Vietnam as divided into North and South by the Geneva Conference of 1954

0   150
Miles

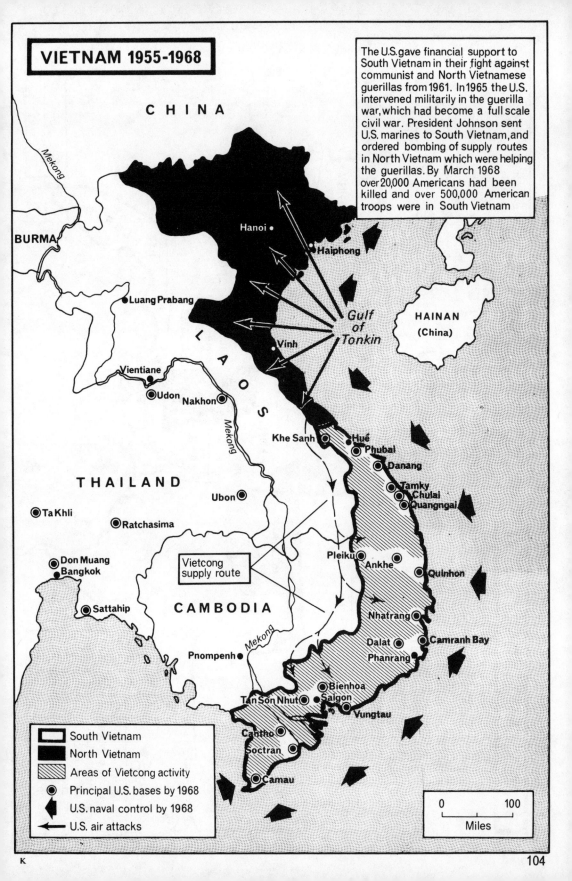

VIETNAM 1955-1968

CHINA

BURMA

Hanoi •

• Haiphong

• Luang Prabang

HAINAN
(China)

L A O S

Vinh •

*Gulf
of
Tonkin*

Vientiane
⊚ Udon Nakhon

Khe Sanh

Hué
Phubal
Danang

T H A I L A N D

Ubon ⊚

Tamky
Chulai
Quangngai

⊚ Ta Khli

⊚ Ratchasima

```
Vietcong
supply route
```

Pleiku •

Ankhe ⊚

⊚ Quinhon

⊚ Don Muang
• Bangkok

C A M B O D I A

Nhatrang ⊚

• Sattahip

Dalat ⊚
Phanrang

⊚ Camranh Bay

Mekong

Pnompenh •

Bienhoa
Tan Son Nhut ⊚
Saigon
Vungtau

Cantho ⊚
Soctran

Camau ⊚

The U.S. gave financial support to
South Vietnam in their fight against
communist and North Vietnamese
guerillas from 1961. In 1965 the U.S.
intervened militarily in the guerilla
war, which had become a full scale
civil war. President Johnson sent
U.S. marines to South Vietnam, and
ordered bombing of supply routes
in North Vietnam which were helping
the guerillas. By March 1968
over 20,000 Americans had been
killed and over 500,000 American
troops were in South Vietnam

▢	South Vietnam
■	North Vietnam
▨	Areas of Vietcong activity
⊚	Principal U.S. bases by 1968
◄	U.S. naval control by 1968
←	U.S. air attacks

```
0          100
Miles
```

K

104

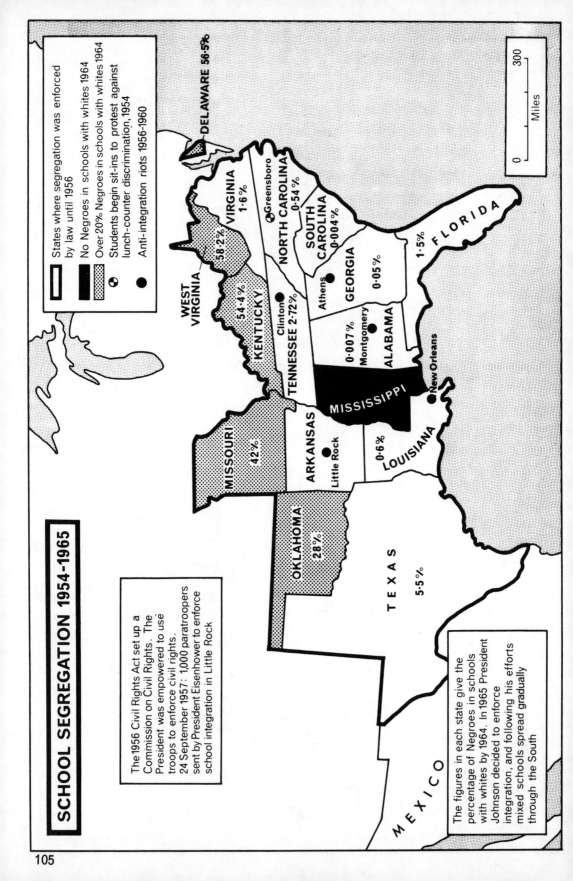

SCHOOL SEGREGATION 1954-1965

States where segregation was enforced by law until 1956

No Negroes in schools with whites 1964

Over 20% Negroes in schools with whites 1964

Students begin sit-ins to protest against lunch-counter discrimination, 1954

Anti-integration riots 1956-1960

The 1956 Civil Rights Act set up a Commission on Civil Rights. The President was empowered to use troops to enforce civil rights.
24 September 1957: 1,000 paratroopers sent by President Eisenhower to enforce school integration in Little Rock

The figures in each state give the percentage of Negroes in schools with whites by 1964. In 1965 President Johnson decided to enforce integration, and following his efforts mixed schools spread gradually through the South

DELAWARE 56·5%

WEST VIRGINIA 58·2%

VIRGINIA 1·6%

Greensboro

NORTH CAROLINA 0·54%

SOUTH CAROLINA 0·004%

FLORIDA 1·5%

KENTUCKY 54·4%

Clinton

TENNESSEE 2·72%

Athens

GEORGIA 0·05%

Montgomery

ALABAMA 0·007%

New Orleans

MISSISSIPPI

MISSOURI 42%

ARKANSAS

Little Rock

LOUISIANA 0·6%

OKLAHOMA 28%

TEXAS 5·5%

MEXICO

0   300
Miles

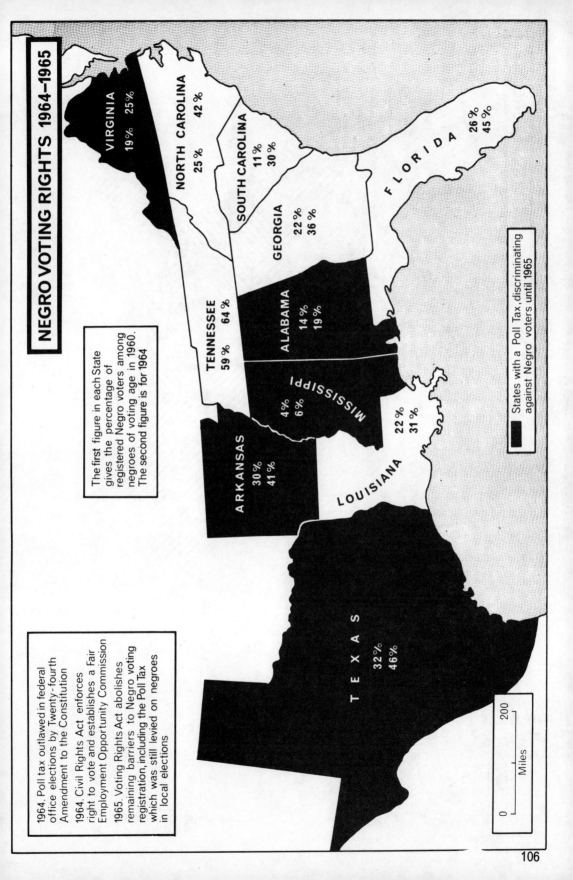

NEGRO VOTING RIGHTS 1964-1965

VIRGINIA
19% 25%

NORTH CAROLINA
25% 42%

SOUTH CAROLINA
11% 30%

GEORGIA
22% 36%

FLORIDA
26% 45%

TENNESSEE
59% 64%

ALABAMA
14% 19%

MISSISSIPPI
4% 6%

ARKANSAS
30% 41%

LOUISIANA
22% 31%

TEXAS
32% 46%

The first figure in each State gives the percentage of registered Negro voters among negroes of voting age in 1960. The second figure is for 1964

1964. Poll tax outlawed in federal office elections by Twenty-fourth Amendment to the Constitution

1964. Civil Rights Act enforces right to vote and establishes a Fair Employment Opportunity Commission

1965. Voting Rights Act abolishes remaining barriers to Negro voting registration, including the Poll Tax which was still levied on negroes in local elections

States with a Poll Tax, discriminating against Negro voters until 1965

0   200
Miles

106

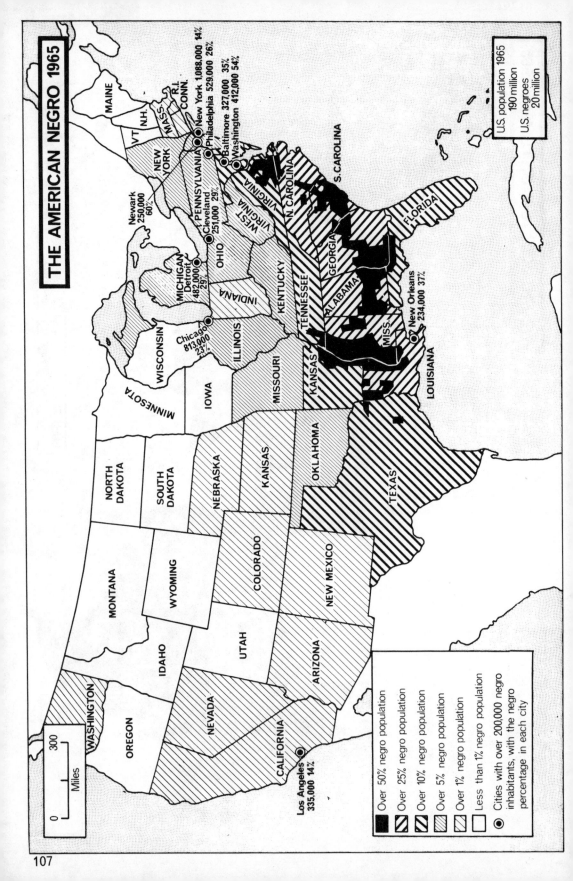

THE AMERICAN NEGRO 1965

U.S. population 1965
190 million
U.S. negroes
20 million

New York 1,088,000 14%
Philadelphia 529,000 26%
Baltimore 327,000 35%
Washington 412,000 54%

Newark 250,000 60%

Cleveland 251,000 29%

Detroit 482,000 29%

Chicago 813,000 23%

New Orleans 234,000 37%

Los Angeles 335,000 14%

MAINE
VT N.H. MASS. R.I. CONN.
NEW YORK
PENNSYLVANIA
WEST VIRGINIA
VIRGINIA
N. CAROLINA
S. CAROLINA
GEORGIA
FLORIDA
ALABAMA
TENNESSEE
KENTUCKY
MISS.
LOUISIANA
MICHIGAN
OHIO
INDIANA
ILLINOIS
WISCONSIN
MINNESOTA
IOWA
MISSOURI
KANSAS
ARKANSAS
OKLAHOMA
TEXAS
NEBRASKA
NORTH DAKOTA
SOUTH DAKOTA
COLORADO
NEW MEXICO
WYOMING
MONTANA
IDAHO
UTAH
ARIZONA
NEVADA
CALIFORNIA
OREGON
WASHINGTON

300
Miles
0

Over 50% negro population
Over 25% negro population
Over 10% negro population
Over 5% negro population
Over 1% negro population
Less than 1% negro population
Cities with over 200,000 negro inhabitants, with the negro percentage in each city

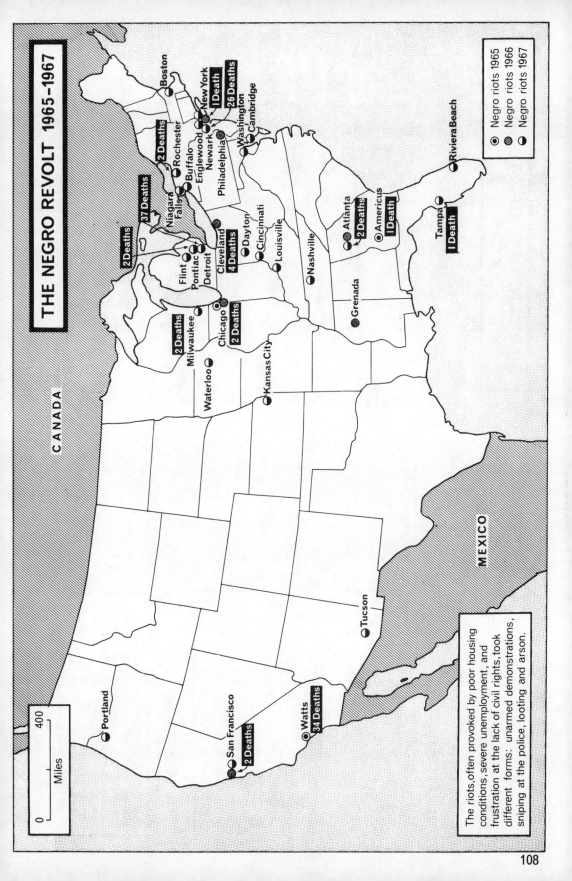

THE NEGRO REVOLT 1965-1967

CANADA

MEXICO

Boston

New York | 1 Death
Newark | 26 Deaths

Rochester | 2 Deaths
Buffalo
Englewood
Washington
Cambridge
Philadelphia

Niagara Falls | 37 Deaths

Dayton
Cincinnati
Cleveland | 4 Deaths
Flint
Pontiac
Detroit | 2 Deaths

Louisville

Nashville

Atlanta | 2 Deaths
Americus | 1 Death

Grenada

Tampa | 1 Death

Riviera Beach

Milwaukee | 2 Deaths
Chicago | 2 Deaths
Waterloo
Kansas City

Tucson

Portland

San Francisco | 2 Deaths

Watts | 34 Deaths

Negro riots 1965
Negro riots 1966
Negro riots 1967

0   400
Miles

The riots, often provoked by poor housing conditions, severe unemployment, and frustration at the lack of civil rights, took different forms: unarmed demonstrations, sniping at the police, looting and arson.

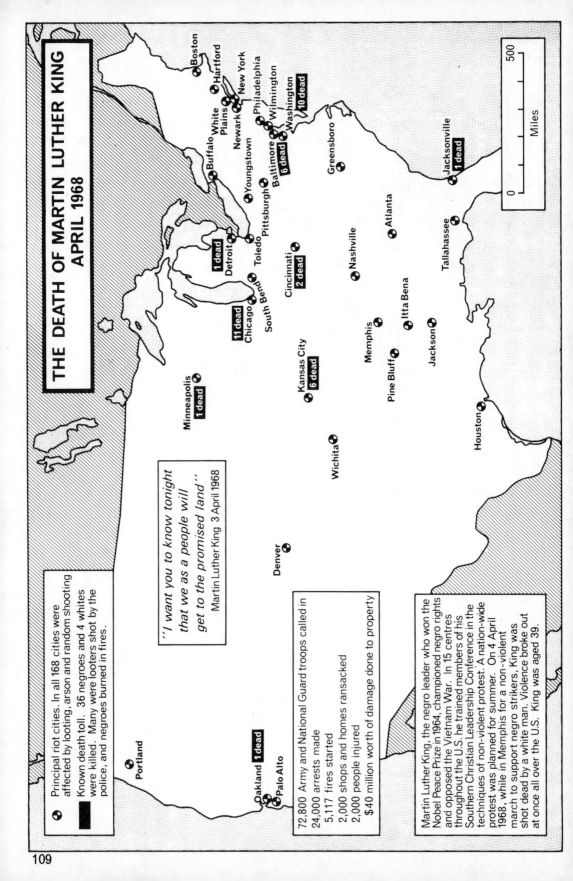

THE DEATH OF MARTIN LUTHER KING
APRIL 1968

Boston

Hartford

White Plains
New York

Buffalo

Philadelphia

Newark

Wilmington

10 dead Washington

Baltimore **6 dead**

Youngstown

Pittsburgh

Greensboro

Jacksonville **1 dead**

1 dead Detroit

Toledo

Atlanta

Cincinnati **2 dead**

Tallahassee

Nashville

South Bend

11 dead Chicago

Itta Bena

Memphis

1 dead Minneapolis

Kansas City **6 dead**

Pine Bluff

Jackson

Wichita

Houston

Denver

Portland

Oakland 1 dead

Palo Alto

0   500
Miles

- ⊕ Principal riot cities. In all 168 cities were affected by looting, arson and random shooting
- ■ Known death toll. 36 negroes and 4 whites were killed. Many were looters shot by the police, and negroes burned in fires.

"I want you to know tonight that we as a people will get to the promised land"
Martin Luther King 3 April 1968

72,800 Army and National Guard troops called in
24,000 arrests made
5,117 fires started
2,000 shops and homes ransacked
2,000 people injured
$40 million worth of damage done to property

Martin Luther King, the negro leader who won the Nobel Peace Prize in 1964, championed negro rights and opposed the U.S. in the Vietnam War. In 15 centres throughout the U.S. he trained members of his Southern Christian Leadership Conference in the techniques of non-violent protest. A nation-wide protest was planned for summer. On 4 April 1968, while in Memphis for a non-violent march to support negro strikers, King was shot dead by a white man. Violence broke out at once all over the U.S. King was aged 39.

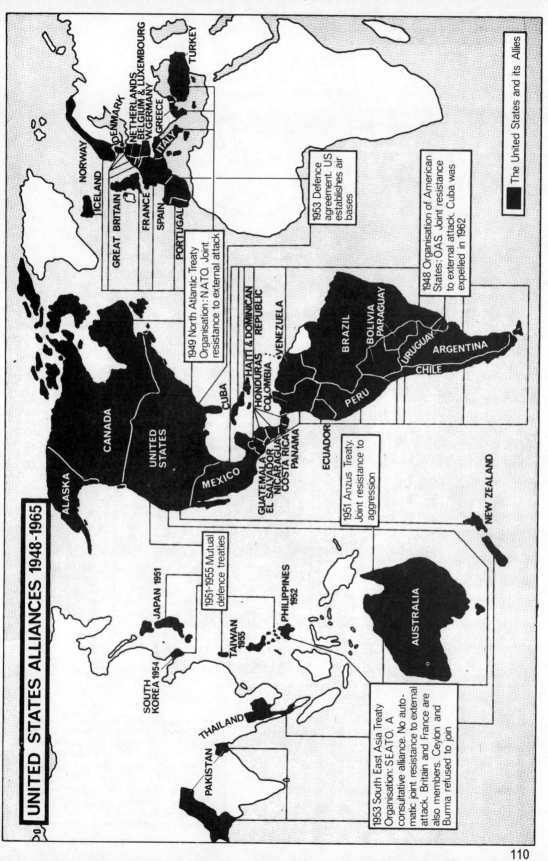

UNITED STATES ALLIANCES 1948-1965

NORWAY
ICELAND
DENMARK
NETHERLANDS
BELGIUM & LUXEMBOURG
W.GERMANY
GREECE
TURKEY
GREAT BRITAIN
FRANCE
SPAIN
ITALY
PORTUGAL

ALASKA
CANADA
UNITED STATES
MEXICO
CUBA
GUATEMALA
EL SALVADOR
NICARAGUA
COSTA RICA
PANAMA
HAITI & DOMINICAN REPUBLIC
HONDURAS
COLOMBIA
VENEZUELA
ECUADOR
PERU
BRAZIL
BOLIVIA
PARAGUAY
CHILE
URUGUAY
ARGENTINA

JAPAN 1951
SOUTH KOREA 1954
TAIWAN 1955
PHILIPPINES 1952
PAKISTAN
THAILAND
AUSTRALIA
NEW ZEALAND

1949 North Atlantic Treaty Organisation: N.A.T.O. Joint resistance to external attack

1953 Defence agreement. US establishes air bases

1948 Organisation of American States: OAS. Joint resistance to external attack. Cuba was expelled in 1962

1951 Anzus Treaty. Joint resistance to aggression

1951-1955 Mutual defence treaties

1953 South East Asia Treaty Organisation: SEATO. A consultative alliance. No auto-matic joint resistance to external attack. Britain and France are also members. Ceylon and Burma refused to join

The United States and its Allies

110

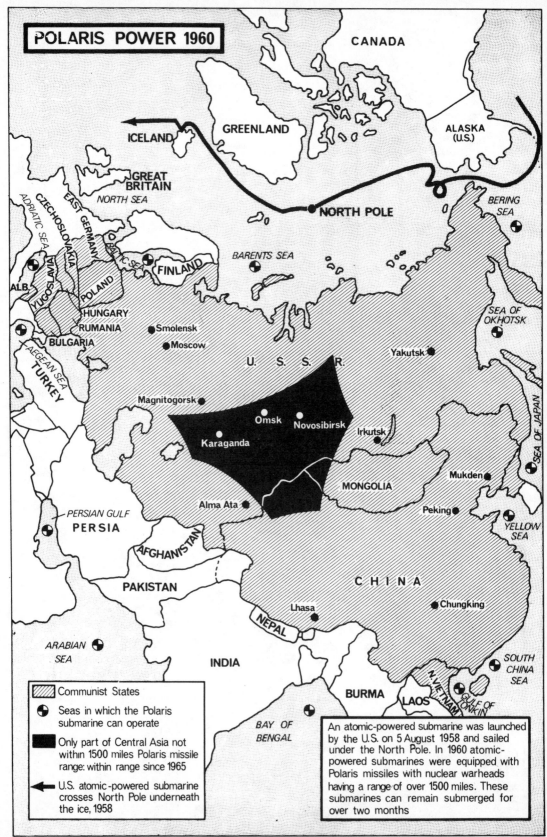

POLARIS POWER 1960

CANADA

GREENLAND

ICELAND

ALASKA (U.S.)

BERING SEA

GREAT BRITAIN

NORTH SEA

EAST GERMANY

CZECHOSLOVAKIA

ADRIATIC SEA

ALB.

YUGOSLAVIA

POLAND

BALTIC SEA

FINLAND

NORTH POLE

BARENTS SEA

SEA OF OKHOTSK

HUNGARY

RUMANIA

BULGARIA

AEGEAN SEA

TURKEY

Smolensk

Moscow

U. S. S. R.

Yakutsk

Magnitogorsk

Omsk

Novosibirsk

Irkutsk

SEA OF JAPAN

Karaganda

Mukden

MONGOLIA

PERSIAN GULF

PERSIA

Alma Ata

Peking

YELLOW SEA

AFGHANISTAN

PAKISTAN

C H I N A

Chungking

NEPAL

Lhasa

ARABIAN SEA

INDIA

BURMA

LAOS

SOUTH CHINA SEA

BAY OF BENGAL

N. VIETNAM

GULF OF TONKIN

Legend

	Communist States
	Seas in which the Polaris submarine can operate
	Only part of Central Asia not within 1500 miles Polaris missile range: within range since 1965
←	U.S. atomic-powered submarine crosses North Pole underneath the ice, 1958

An atomic-powered submarine was launched by the U.S. on 5 August 1958 and sailed under the North Pole. In 1960 atomic-powered submarines were equipped with Polaris missiles with nuclear warheads having a range of over 1500 miles. These submarines can remain submerged for over two months

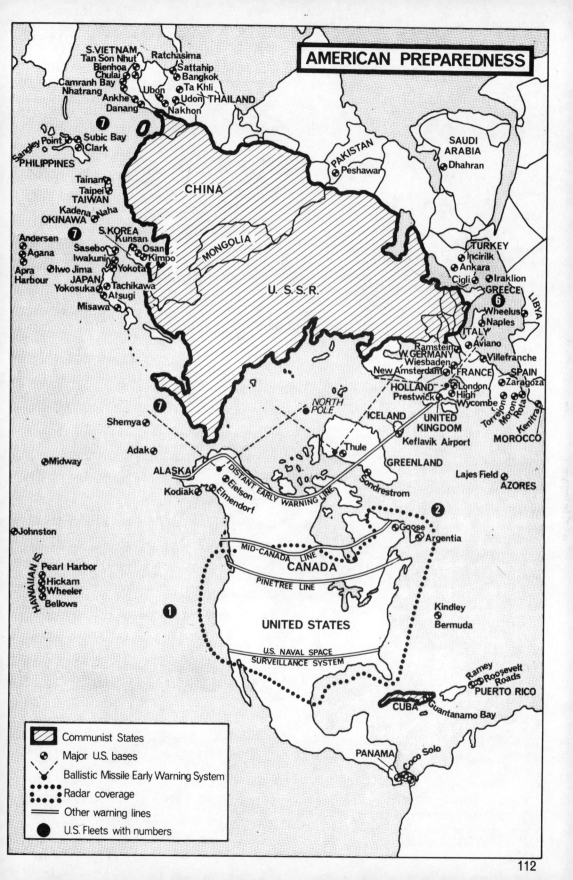

AMERICAN PREPAREDNESS

S.VIETNAM
Tan Son Nhut
Bienhoa · Ratchasima
Chulai · Sattahip
Camranh Bay · Bangkok
Nhatrang · Ta Khli
· Ubon · Udon THAILAND
Ankhe · Nakhon
Danang

PHILIPPINES
Sangley Point · Subic Bay
· Clark

Tainan
Taipei
TAIWAN

Kadena · Naha
OKINAWA
S.KOREA
Kunsan
Andersen · Osan
Agana Sasebo · Kimpo
Iwakuni
Apra Iwo Jima · Yokota
Harbour JAPAN
Yokosuka · Tachikawa
Atsugi
Misawa

CHINA

MONGOLIA

U.S.S.R.

PAKISTAN
· Peshawar

SAUDI
ARABIA
· Dhahran

TURKEY
· Incirlik
· Ankara
Cigli · Iraklion
GREECE
Wheelus
· Naples
ITALY
Ramstein · Aviano
W.GERMANY
Wiesbaden · Villefranche
New Amsterdam FRANCE
HOLLAND · SPAIN
London · Zaragoza
Prestwick · High
· Wycombe
UNITED
ICELAND KINGDOM
Keflavik Airport
MOROCCO
Torrejon · Rota
Moron · Kenitra

LIBYA

Shemya

NORTH
POLE

Thule

GREENLAND

Sondrestrom

Lajes Field
AZORES

Adak

Midway

ALASKA
DISTANT EARLY WARNING LINE
Kodiak · Eielson
· Elmendorf

Johnston

Goose
Argentia

MID-CANADA LINE
CANADA
PINETREE LINE

HAWAIIAN IS.
Pearl Harbor
Hickam
Wheeler
Bellows

UNITED STATES

Kindley
Bermuda

U.S. NAVAL SPACE
SURVEILLANCE SYSTEM

Ramey · Roosevelt
Roads
PUERTO RICO

CUBA · Guantanamo Bay

PANAMA · Coco Solo

	Communist States
	Major U.S. bases
	Ballistic Missile Early Warning System
	Radar coverage
	Other warning lines
	U.S. Fleets with numbers

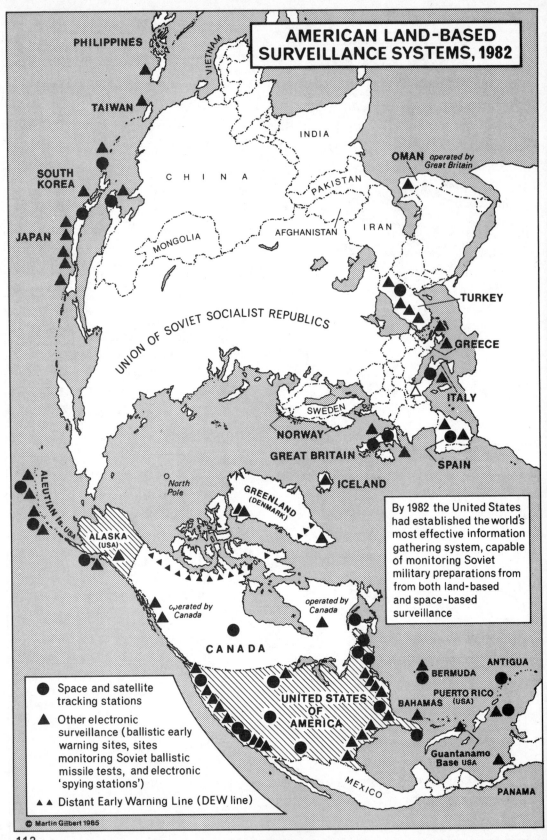

AMERICAN LAND-BASED SURVEILLANCE SYSTEMS, 1982

PHILIPPINES

TAIWAN

SOUTH KOREA

JAPAN

ALEUTIAN Is USA

VIETNAM

CHINA

INDIA

MONGOLIA

AFGHANISTAN

PAKISTAN

IRAN

OMAN *operated by Great Britain*

TURKEY

GREECE

ITALY

UNION OF SOVIET SOCIALIST REPUBLICS

SPAIN

SWEDEN

NORWAY

GREAT BRITAIN

North Pole

GREENLAND (DENMARK)

ICELAND

ALASKA (USA)

operated by Canada

operated by Canada

CANADA

BERMUDA

ANTIGUA

PUERTO RICO (USA)

BAHAMAS

UNITED STATES OF AMERICA

Guantanamo Base USA

MEXICO

PANAMA

By 1982 the United States had established the world's most effective information gathering system, capable of monitoring Soviet military preparations from from both land-based and space-based surveillance

● Space and satellite tracking stations

▲ Other electronic surveillance (ballistic early warning sites, sites monitoring Soviet ballistic missile tests, and electronic 'spying stations')

▲▲ Distant Early Warning Line (DEW line)

© Martin Gilbert 1985

113

THE UNITED STATES AND THE SOVIET UNION IN OUTER SPACE

Between 1957 and 1981 a total of 2,725 satellites were launched, most of them by the United States and the Soviet Union. Some of the principal satellites in orbit in 1981 are shown here. In March 1981 the US National Aeronautics and Space Administration (NASA) launched its Columbia Orbiter, the first re-usable space vehicle (44 missions planned by the end of 1985, nine of them military)

SATELLITES

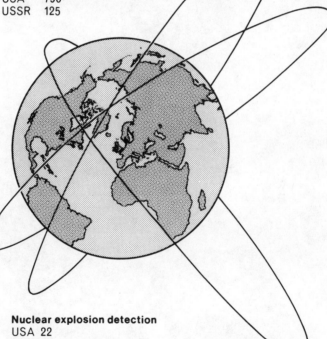

Early Warning
USA 22
USSR 25

Photographic reconnaisance
USA 235
USSR 538
China 3

Communications
USA 118
USSR 366
NATO 5
UK 4
France 2

Electronic reconnaisance
USA 790
USSR 125

Navigation
USA 39
USSR 25

Nuclear explosion detection
USA 22

Ocean surveillance
USA 18
USSR 32

Interception-destruction
USSR 33

In January 1985, at Geneva, the United States and the Soviet Union agreed to begin talks aimed at an agreement over the restriction of warfare in outer space. The United States was involved in the development of anti-satellite missiles and anti-missile lasers, and the Soviet Union in anti-satellite satellites

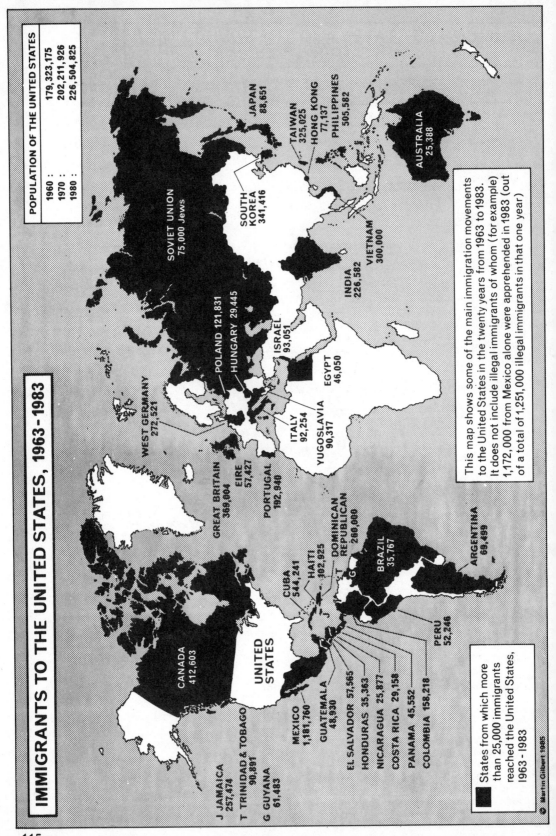

IMMIGRANTS TO THE UNITED STATES, 1963-1983

POPULATION OF THE UNITED STATES

1960 : 179,323,175
1970 : 202,211,926
1980 : 226,504,825

JAPAN 88,651

TAIWAN 325,025

HONG KONG 77,137

PHILIPPINES 505,582

AUSTRALIA 25,388

SOVIET UNION 75,000 Jews

SOUTH KOREA 341,416

VIETNAM 300,000

INDIA 226,582

POLAND 121,831

HUNGARY 29,445

ISRAEL 93,051

EGYPT 46,050

WEST GERMANY 272,521

ITALY 92,254

YUGOSLAVIA 90,317

GREAT BRITAIN 369,904

EIRE 57,427

PORTUGAL 192,940

DOMINICAN REPUBLIC 260,000

BRAZIL 35,767

ARGENTINA 68,499

CUBA 544,241

HAITI 102,925

PERU 52,246

CANADA 412,603

UNITED STATES

MEXICO 1,181,760

GUATEMALA 48,930

EL SALVADOR 57,565

HONDURAS 35,363

NICARAGUA 25,877

COSTA RICA 29,158

PANAMA 45,552

COLOMBIA 158,218

J JAMAICA 257,474

T TRINIDAD & TOBAGO 90,891

G GUYANA 61,483

This map shows some of the main immigration movements to the United States in the twenty years from 1963 to 1983. It does not include illegal immigrants of whom (for example) 1,172,000 from Mexico alone were apprehended in 1983 (out of a total of 1,251,000 illegal immigrants in that one year)

States from which more than 25,000 immigrants reached the United States, 1963 - 1983

© Martin Gilbert 1985

115